The Force of Spirit

Also by Scott Russell Sanders

nonfiction   The Country of Language

Hunting for Hope

Writing from the Center

Staying Put

Secrets of the Universe

The Paradise of Bombs

In Limestone Country

Audubon Reader (as editor)

D. H. Lawrence

fiction   The Invisible Company

The Engineer of Beasts

Bad Man Ballad

Terrarium

Wonders Hidden

Fetching the Dead

Wilderness Plots

for children   Crawdad Creek

Meeting Trees

A Place Called Freedom

The Floating House

Here Comes the Mystery Man

Warm as Wool

Aurora Means Dawn

Hear the Wind Blow

The Force of Spirit

Scott Russell Sanders

Beacon Press
Boston

Beacon Press
25 Beacon Street
Boston, Massachusetts 02108-2892
www.beacon.org

Beacon Press books
are published under the auspices of
the Unitarian Universalist Association of Congregations.

Printed in the United States of America

05 04 03 02 01 00   8 7 6 5 4 3 2 1

This book is printed on acid-free paper that meets the uncoated paper
ANSI/NISO specifications for permanence as revised in 1992.

Text design by Sara Eisenman
Composition by Wilsted & Taylor Publishing Services

Library of Congress Cataloging-in-Publication Data

Sanders, Scott R. (Scott Russell).
    The force of spirit / Scott Russell Sanders.
        p.   cm.
    Includes bibliographical references (p.).
    ISBN 0-8070-6296-0 (cl)
    1. Sanders, Scott R. (Scott Russell).   2. Authors, American—20th
century—Biography.   I. Title.
PS3569.A5137 Z468   2000
818'.5409—dc21
    [B]   00-031141

for John Elder   *What could be sweeter*

than to have a friend

with whom, as with

yourself, you can discuss

all that is in your heart?

—Meister Eckhart

Summon the rare word

for the rare desire.

—James Wright

The search may begin

with a restless feeling, as

if one were being watched.

One turns in all directions

and sees nothing. Yet

one senses that there is a

source for this deep

restlessness, and the path

that leads there is not a

path to a strange place,

but the path home.

—Peter Matthiessen

Contents

Introduction

While these essays grew from seeds of bewilderment and wonder, I entered my second half-century, and the world, by common reckoning, entered a new millennium. Fifty and 2000 are only numbers, but they are round and full enough to have made me keenly aware of time passing.

Events in my life reinforced the lesson. During the writing of this book, my two children moved out of our house, graduated from college, married, and started households of their own. My wife's father suffered a series of strokes, and her mother died. I could no longer provide everything my own mother needed to stay in the house where she had lived since my father's death, so I helped move her into an apartment, which meant persuading her to let go of many possessions. Meanwhile, my wife and I increased our own possessions, buying country land and building a cabin there. By acquiring a camp in the woods I fulfilled one childhood dream, even while I was relinquishing others—the dream of becoming a physicist or a musician, of mastering several languages, of living between the mountains and the sea, of running a greenhouse, of saving my soul.

Wisdom comes, if it comes at all, not only by the accumulation of experience, but also by the letting go, by the paring away of dross until only essentials remain. I have reached the time in life when I can no longer put off asking the ultimate questions.

Where are we, in what sort of universe? Is there a pattern in the confusion of details? How did we come to be here, and why? What is our place among the other creatures? How should we spend our modest allowance of time? The obvious risk is that my answers will be too small, too clumsy, an amateur's raid on mystery; but that is less of a risk than to leave the questions unasked.

Once there's food on the table, clothes on one's back, a roof over one's head, and once the children are standing on their own feet, the main task remaining is to figure out what it all means. Is life merely a passing-on of genes, like the pointless grinding of a perpetual-motion machine, forever running but going nowhere? Is life a trick played on matter by a capricious god? Is it a cosmic accident, signifying nothing? Or is life a school? And if so, who or what is the teacher, what are we supposed to learn, and what should we do with our knowledge?

In struggling with these questions, I have come to appreciate more fully why the remarkable sixteenth-century French writer Michel de Montaigne chose to call this literary form he invented an *essai*, by which he meant a trial or experiment, an effort at making sense. The deeper I go into my days, the more I'm convinced that living itself is an experiment. Life keeps confronting me with puzzles that I can neither ignore nor easily solve. I am moved to write essays not because I understand so much but because I understand so little.

The world appears to be a vast whirl of bits and pieces, yet scientists operate on the belief that behind this dazzling variety there is a single set of laws, and a single energy, at play in the universe. Religion makes the same assumption, although it offers quite different explanations for those laws, tells quite different stories about that energy. The word *religion* derives from *re-* plus *ligare,* meaning to bind back together, as if things have been scattered and now must be gathered again. That is the rhythm of my days—a scattering and gathering, scattering and gathering. The writing of essays allows me to gather what is essential in my life, and by pondering these things perhaps to discover something essential to the lives of others.

In trying to show what binds together the seeming scatter of things, I find myself pointing to an elusive energy, a shaping power that flashes forth in nature, in gesture, in human speech and action. And when I glimpse it, I can do little more than cry, "There it is!" All the names we use for the fire at the heart of matter are risky—God, Yahweh, Creator, Allah, Manitou, among countless others—for each comes freighted with a long, compromising history. From all the possible names I favor *spirit,* because the word seems to catch the lightness, radiance, and windlike subtlety of the power that I seek.

This power seeks me, as well, or so it seems, for time and again I feel the pressure of an inescapable force that is sometimes delicate, like a wing brushing my face, and sometimes fierce, like a hand squeezing my heart. I cannot predict when this force will visit me, any more than I can say when the red-tailed hawk that hunts from the ridge behind our cabin will kite across the sky. I can only watch and wait and make these offerings of words.

The Force of Spirit

My wife's father is dying, and I can think of little else, because I love him and I love my wife. Once or twice a week, Ruth and I drive the forty miles of winding roads to visit him in the nursing home. Along the way we pass fields bursting with new corn, stands of trees heavy with fresh leaves, pastures deep in grass. In that long grass the lambs and calves and colts hunt for tender shoots to nibble and for the wet nipples of their mothers to suck. The meadows are thick with flowers, and butterflies waft over the blossoms like petals torn loose by wind. The spring this year was lavish, free of late frosts, well soaked with rain, and now in early June the Indiana countryside is all juiced up.

On our trip to the nursing home this morning, I drive while Ruth sits beside me knitting. Strand by strand, a sweater grows under her hands. We don't talk much, because she must keep count of her stitches. To shape the silence, we play a tape of Mozart's Requiem from a recent concert in which Ruth sang, and I try to detect her clear soprano in the weave of voices. The car fills with the music of sorrow. The sound rouses aches in me from earlier losses, the way cold rouses pain from old bone breaks.

Yet when I look out through the windows at the blaze of sunlight and the blast of green, I forget for minutes at a time where we're going and what we're likely to see when we get there. Ruth must forget as well, because every now and again she glances up from her knitting to recall a story or a task or some odd discovery she's read about recently.

As we slow down for a hamlet named Cope—a cluster of frame houses gathered at a bend in the road—she describes a scientific article that she came across at the lab this past week. The author, a biologist, was puzzling over what distinguishes living organisms from dead matter, she tells me, and after years of experiments he concluded that the vital secret is the flow of electrons in association with oxygen.

I tell her that all sounds reasonable enough, but I wonder why oxygen goes hauling electrons around in the first place.

"He hasn't figured that out yet," she replies.

"Wouldn't it be easier," I say, "for oxygen to sit still and leave matter alone? Why stir things up?"

"In other words, why life?"

"Yeah, why life?"

She laughs. "Ask me an easy one."

"Think about it," I say. "Why corn? Why shagbark hickories? Why moss and wolves? Why not just rock and dust?"

Used to my pestering her with questions, Ruth normally answers with good humor and patience. But now she merely says, "You'll have to read the article."

A fly beats against the inside of the windshield. Suddenly the crazed, buzzing bit of stuff seems bizarre and precious. I lift one hand from the steering wheel, crank down a window, shoo the fly to freedom, then grip the wheel once more. Now my fingers seem utterly strange. How can they curl so exactly in the shape of my thoughts? The lurching of my heart surprises me, as if a desperate animal has crawled inside my chest. All at once my whole body feels like an implausible contraption, and my skin barely contains the storm of electrons.

What I feel is not exactly panic, because I'm spared for the moment the chill of knowing I will die. What I feel right now is amazement that anything lives, fly or hawk, virus or man. The radiant fields and woods flowing past our windows seem far-fetched, outrageous. Why all those leaves waving? Why all those juicy stems thrusting at the sky? Why those silky black wings of crows slicing the air? And why am I set moving through this luminous world, only to feel such grief when some patch of woods falls before the saw, when a farm vanishes beneath the pavement of a shopping mall or a valley beneath a reservoir, when a man withers in a nursing home bed?

"What are you thinking?" I ask Ruth, just to hear her voice.

"I'm thinking I only need two more inches to finish the front of this sweater."

"About your dad, I mean."

She turns her brown eyes on me, reading my face, which has grown transparent to her gaze over thirty years of marriage. Her own heart-shaped face draws into a frown. "I'm wondering if he'll still know us."

"Surely he's not that far gone," I say.

"Maybe not yet," she agrees.

I turn my attention back to the music, and gradually Mozart restores my composure.

After a while Ruth sets down her knitting and takes up a stack of her father's insurance papers. She's been working on them for months, yet the stack keeps growing thicker, each layer of papers recording another bout in the hospital, another round of tests. She circles numbers, places checkmarks beside dates, compares one statement with another, imposing order on this chronicle of illness. Congestive heart failure is the short name for what afflicts him. After coronary seizures, quadruple bypass surgery, the insertion of a pacemaker, and several strokes, and after seventy-eight years of faithfully pumping blood, Earl McClure's heart is simply wearing out.

Every now and again as she works on the insurance forms, Ruth sighs, whether because of the tedious papers, or because of the history they record, I can't tell.

Near a tiny settlement called Bud, we pass a white barn that bears a warning in letters six feet high: AT THE END THERE IS JUDGMENT! One side of the barn is painted with the silhouette of a man hanging on a cross, the figure entirely black except for two white rings marking the eyes, which glare out like searchlights. A caption explains, HE DIED FOR YOU.

Ruth and I have known since childhood who he is, this dangling man, for we both spent nearly all of our childhood Sundays in Methodist churches, singing hymns, memorizing Bible verses, listening to sermons, learning that Jesus saves. Although Ruth still sings regularly in a church choir and I sit in a pew on the occasional Sunday with a Bible in my lap, neither of us any longer feels confident that the man on the cross will preserve us from annihilation, nor that he will reunite us with our loved ones in heaven. The only meetings we count on are those we make in the flesh. The only time we're sure of is right now.

"Whenever we pass by here," Ruth says, "I wonder why anybody would paint such a scary picture on a barn. Who'd want to look every day at those awful eyes?"

"They're meant to keep your mind on ultimate things as you milk the cows."

"They're creepy," she insists.

I agree, but I also understand the attraction of a faith that eases the sting of loss, including the loss of one's own precious life. Until I was twenty or so I embraced that faith, hoping for heaven, then I gradually surrendered it under the assault of science, and in dismay over witnessing so much evil carried out in Christ's name. I no longer believe that Jesus can do our dying for us; we must do that for ourselves, one by one. Yet I've not given up believing in the power that reportedly sent him to redeem us, the Creator who laid the foundations of the world.

For the last few miles of our drive to the nursing home, I study the land. There's a shaping intelligence at work here, I feel sure of it. I sense a magnificent energy in the grasses bowing beneath the wind, in the butterflies flouncing from blossom to blossom, in the trees reaching skyward and the jays haranguing from the topmost branches and the clouds fluffing by. I sense in this rippling countryside a tremendous throb and surge, the same force that squeezes and relaxes my heart. Everything rides on one current. As I listen to the music of grief filling the car, as I go with my wife to visit her dying father, the world, for all its density and weight, seems made of breath.

Legend has it that Mozart died while composing his Requiem, a few measures into the section beginning with the Latin word *lacrimosa*, which means tearful or weeping. "On that day of weeping," the verse proclaims,

> *again from the ashes will arise*
> *guilty mankind, to be judged.*

That much he orchestrated, but he never completed the remainder of the verse:

Therefore, spare this one, O God,

Merciful Lord Jesus,

And grant them rest.

Ostensibly, the one to be spared from God's wrath was the dearly departed wife of the count who had commissioned this Mass for the Dead, but the ailing Mozart must also have been mourning himself. Another scrap of legend claims that in his final days he said, "It is for myself that I am writing this." I suspect he was grieving as well for his own dearly departed, especially his mother, who had died some years earlier in Paris while he was there looking for work.

Ruth's mother died last October, not long before the chorus began rehearsing the Requiem. By the time of her death, Dessa McClure had been whittled away for half a dozen years by Alzheimer's disease, losing her memory, speech, balance, and strength, becoming again as a little child. This was not the sort of child she had aspired to become, for she meant to find her way to heaven by achieving a clear vision and a simple heart. Toward the end, her vision grew cloudy, and the world became a blur of strange rooms and unknown faces. And at the very end, while she was rising from a bath, her heart quit.

The nurse who'd been helping her at the time told us afterward, "She went limp all of a sudden and dropped right down and was gone."

Ruth's father, still able to get around fairly well back then, had just been to see Dessa in the special care unit, where patients suffering from various forms of dementia drifted about like husks blown by an idle breeze. She had seemed almost happy, he recalled. She even whistled a bit, and showed no signs of pain. And he was sure she'd recognized him by the way she squeezed his finger and smiled. He let that be his last glimpse of her, for he chose not to look at his wife's body after the nurses brought him news of her death.

But Ruth saw her laid out in the nursing home, still crumpled, as if, when breath departed, the body had collapsed like an empty sack. Ruth was so appalled by the image that she insisted on seeing her mother's body one more time before the cremation. And so, after we had finished our business in the funeral home, she and I slipped into a back room to gaze for a moment at the shell of her mother resting on a cart, all but the face hidden by a white sheet, the skin pale except for dark rings under the shut eyes. We knew this face, yet it seemed aloof and slack, for it had been peeled away from the person to whom it once belonged. Beneath the sheet, the body lay as motionless as a piece of furniture covered with drapery in a vacant house. I put my arm around Ruth, not so much to comfort her as to comfort me, to feel the warmth and weight of her. She tilted her head against my shoulder and stood there for a long while without speaking. Then she leaned forward, ran a hand over that forsaken face, and turned to go.

The heart is only a muscle. It's a meaty pump that shoves and sucks the blood that carries the oxygen that hauls the electrons that keep us alive. It beats forty or a hundred and forty times a minute, hour after hour, day after day, until, between one contraction and the next, it falters and stops. When surgeons lay the heart open to repair valves and carve out damaged tissue, they find no spirit hiding there, no seat of the soul. Biologists can trace it back down the evolutionary path to the earliest twitchings of life in the sea.

Yet who can accept that we're merely meat? Who can shake the suspicion that we're more than two-legged heaps of dust accidentally sprung into motion? Whatever the doctors and biologists claim, we go on using the word *heart* as if it pointed to an emotional center, a core of integrity. We trust those who speak from the heart. We're wary of those who are heartless and hardhearted. Have a heart, we say, begging for kindness. Home is where the heart is, we say. We're drawn irresistibly to our heart throb, who knows how to pluck our heartstrings. We long to feel heartsease by fulfilling our heart's desire. In our earnest pronouncements, we appeal to hearts and minds, heart and soul. Swearing most solemnly, we cross our hearts and hope to die, if what we say should be a lie. Heartfelt and heartsick, heartland and heartache, heartwood and heartbreak: the word, like the muscle beating in our chest, is indispensable. The beliefs we truly live by, the ones we'll die for, are those we hold in our heart of hearts.

At the nursing home, we find Ruth's father drowsing on his bed, arms outstretched as if he has fallen there from a great height. He wears a white shirt, brown dress pants, low knit socks that leave his ankles bare, and lace-up leather shoes. His hair, still dark and full, is neatly combed. Except for his gauntness, he might be a man resting after a day at the office. Yet he's too frail even to stand up for more than a few minutes at a time. His wrists are sticks. His cheeks are hollow. Blue veins show through the translucent skin of his jaw.

I can see Ruth hesitate before waking him, because she wonders if he will recognize her. So long as he sleeps, she remains his daughter. At last she lightly touches one of those out-flung arms, and he startles awake. Behind thick spectacles, his eyes are milky and uncertain. He looks bewildered for a moment, and then he beams, reaching out to grasp Ruth's hand.

"Hey, there," he says. "I'd about given up on you."

"Don't you worry," she answers. "If I say I'm coming, I'm coming."

"Well, I was thinking . . ." he begins, then loses his way and falls silent with an embarrassed little shrug.

But he has said enough to assure Ruth that he knows her, that he's still there in his withered body. She asks how he's feeling, how he's eating, whether he's had any visitors, whether the nurses have been treating him well, and he answers each question in two or three words, staring up into her face and squeezing her hand.

To say that he is dying makes it sound as though he's doing something active, like singing or dancing, but really something's being done to him. Life is leaving him. From one visit to the next we can see it withdrawing, inch by inch, the way the tide retreating down a beach leaves behind dry sand. With each passing day he has more and more trouble completing sentences, as if words, too, were abandoning him.

I hang back, awkward before his terrible weakness. Eventually he notices me standing near the foot of his bed.

"Why, here's Scott," he says.

I step closer. "I came to see if you're behaving yourself."

"I am, pretty much," he says. "How was the drive over?"

"It was beautiful," I tell him, lifting my voice because I can see he's left his hearing aids in a dish on the bedside table. "Everything's blooming. The corn's shooting up. Some of the hay is cut and drying."

"Good, good," he murmurs. Then he asks if I've been watching the NBA tournament, which I haven't, and so he tells me, pausing for breath between sentences, how the Indiana Pacers lost a play-off game to the New York Knicks. The Pacers had a lead going into the fourth quarter, but their legs gave out. "I understand tired legs," he says, and gives a wheezy laugh.

Ruth and I exchange looks, amazed that he's following basketball. He's also following our children, Eva and Jesse, for now he asks what they've been up to since our last visit. After we tell him, he repeats what we've said, as if to pin down memory: "So Jesse's working in the restaurant. Is that right? Eva's studying birds? She bought a new computer?" His voice is thin and soft, like a trickle of water over smooth stone.

Since we saw him last, Ruth and I have attended a college graduation in Ohio. He remembers this as well, and asks if we had a good time. We did, I answer. And then I tell him about watching the graduates troop across the stage as each name was called, most of them so young and spry they fairly danced in their black robes, while parents and friends and fellow students cheered. A few waddled heavily or limped stiffly. Two scooted across in electric chairs. Then near the end of the ceremony, one slight woman who'd been waiting in line among those receiving degrees in nursing rose from a wheelchair, labored up the stairs, and slowly crossed the stage while holding on to the arm of a young man. When the president gave her the diploma and shook her hand, the audience broke out in the loudest applause of the afternoon. We clapped because many of us knew she was gravely ill with cancer, she'd not been expected to live until commencement, and yet she'd refused to give up. Now here she was, on stage for a moment, drawing our praise.

When I finish my story, which poured out of me before I thought how it might sound in the ears of a dying man, Ruth's father says, "She's got spunk."

"She does," I agree.

"I like that," he says. "You can never have too much spunk." He rouses a bit to report that he's going once a day to physical therapy. They wheel him down there in his chair, but then they make him stand up and push a walker across the room to build up his legs, and make him lift dumbbells to build up his arms.

"Pumping iron, are you?" I say.

"I need to get my strength back." He raises an arm and the sleeve droops down, revealing the tender bruised skin of his wrist.

We learned from a doctor this week that his heart now pumps blood at twenty percent of the normal rate, and it will keep on dwindling. His eyes close, but he doesn't let go of Ruth's hand. She says we'd better let him get some rest. Does he need anything before we go? Yes, he answers, three things: his bathrobe, an extra pair of trousers, and his electric shaver.

I go to fetch them from his apartment on the floor below, a comfortable suite of rooms where he's never likely to stay by himself again. Going there and coming back, I take the stairs two at a time. I rush down the halls past elderly residents who look at me as if I'm a lunatic. There's no reason to race, except that I still can, and so I do, savoring the bounce in my legs and the wild flutter in my chest.

I want a name for the force that keeps Earl McClure asking questions while the tide of life withdraws from him. I want a name for the force that abandoned the body of Dessa McClure and left it like a piece of shrouded furniture on a cart in the funeral home. I want a name for the force that carried a woman dying of cancer through her studies and across a stage to claim her diploma. I want a name for the force that binds me to Ruth, to her parents, to my parents, to our children, to neighbors and friends, to the land and all its creatures.

This power is larger than life, although it contains life. It's tougher than love, although it contains love. It's akin to the power I sense in lambs nudging the teats of their dams to bring down milk, in the raucous tumult of crows high in trees, in the splendor of leaves gorging on sun. I recognize this force at work in children puzzling over a new fact, in grown-ups welcoming strangers, in our capacity, young and old, for laughter and kindness, for mercy and imagination.

No name is large enough to hold this power, but of all the inadequate names, the one that comes to me now is spirit. I know the risks of using such a churchy word. Believers may find me blasphemous for speaking of the wind that blows through all things without tracing the breath to God. Nonbelievers may find me superstitious for invoking any force beyond gravity, electromagnetism, and the binding energy of atoms. But I must run those risks, for I cannot understand the world, cannot understand my life, without appealing to the force of spirit. If what I feel for my wife or her father and mother is only a by-product of hormones, then what I feel for swift rivers or slow turtles, for the shivering call of a screech owl or the green thrust of bloodroot breaking ground, is equally foolish. If we and the creatures who share the earth with us are only bundles of quarks in motion, however intricate or clever the shapes, then our affection for one another, our concern for other species, our devotion to wildness, our longing for union with the Creation are all mere delusions.

I can't prove it, but I believe we're more than accidental bundles of quarks, more than matter in motion. Our fellowship with other creatures is real, our union with the Creation is already achieved, because we all rise and fall on a single breath. You and I and the black-footed ferret, the earth, the sun, and the far-flung galaxies are dust motes whirling in the same great wind. Whether we call that magnificent energy Spirit or Tao, Creator or God, Allah or Atman or some other holy name, or no name at all, makes little difference so long as we honor it. Wherever it flows—in person or place, in animal or plant or the whole of nature—we feel the pressure of the sacred, and that alone deserves our devotion.

A gusty breeze is pawing the grass and churning the ponds as Ruth and I drive back from the nursing home over the winding roads. Neither of us can bear to hear the Requiem again right now, so we talk. She remembers stories of her father from when he was strong—how he lifted her in and out of bed when she was down with rheumatic fever, how he laid fires in a charcoal grill when the family went camping, how he dug up the yard to plant roses. She recalls how, in their last house before the nursing home, her father and mother used to stand spellbound at the dining room window and watch birds at the feeders. And she recalls how, even in the final stark days, her mother shuffled to the bird-cage in the special care unit and watched the fierce, tiny finches darting about, squabbling and courting. From inside the Alzheimer's daze, her mother would say nothing, but sometimes she whistled at the finches, and sometimes she laughed.

As if summoned by these memories of Dessa and Earl Mc-Clure, birds fill this blustery June afternoon here in southern Indiana. We see goldfinches dipping and rising as they graze among the waving seed heads of the tall grasses. We see red-winged blackbirds clinging to the tops of cattails that sway in the breeze. We see a kettle of hawks, a swirl of starlings, a fluster of crows. A great blue heron goes beating by, and six or eight geese plow the ruffled waters of a lake. Near the barn that's painted with the crucified man, more than a dozen turkey vultures spiral over a field, a lazy black funnel pointing down toward carrion.

There's an abundance in this teeming land that promises to make up for anything lost to vultures. The corn seems to have shot up higher since our drive over this morning. In the afternoon heat the woods bristle and the pastures heave and the fields are charged with light.

After a while Ruth takes up her knitting, clacks along for a few stitches, then puts it down again. Gazing out the window, she recalls in a soft voice how she thought of her mother at every rehearsal of the Requiem, and how moved she was at the performance itself when the conductor announced that the concert would be given in memory of Dessa McClure. Ruth had been forewarned of this gesture, but still she had to blink hard to read the opening measures.

We pass a hayfield where a tractor is rolling the cut grass into fat round bales, and I can't help thinking of the verse in Isaiah:

All flesh is grass,
    and all its beauty is like the flower of the field.

The grass withers, the flower fades,
  when the breath of the Lord blows upon it;
surely the people is grass.

These days, I'm in no danger of forgetting how swiftly every living thing withers. But I also remember that grass, once cut, sprouts up again from the roots. Whatever Lord breathes upon this world of crickets and constellations blows beginnings as well as endings. The Latin word for breath is *spiritus,* which also means courage, air, and life. Our own word *spirit* carries all those overtones for me when I use it to speak of the current that lifts us into this life and bears us along and eventually lets us go.

We pass more fields scattered with round bales of hay like herds of slow, ungainly beasts. When we draw up behind a truck that sags under the weight of a single great bale, a stream of chaff comes blowing back at us, and loose bits float in through our open windows.

I reach over to brush some straw from Ruth's lap. She grabs my hand and holds on.

"I hate to think of clearing out Daddy's things," she says. "We'll have to find who wants what, then get rid of the rest."

"Let's hope that won't be for a while yet," I say.

She doesn't answer. We drive on through the lush green countryside. I remember when we cleared out Dessa's things, how we found more than forty Bibles and hundreds upon hundreds of religious books, which she had long since lost the ability to read. In drawers and cupboards and closets we found entry forms for sweepstakes, because she had decided, as her mind began to go, that winning some game of chance might set things right. And we found lists she had made of crucial events in her life—her marriage, her children's births, her surgeries, her husband's heart attack, the death of her parents, the moves from house to house— all the personal history that was slipping away from her. On page after page in a spiral notebook she wrote down in broken phrases what mattered to her, what defined her life, as if words on paper might preserve what the mind no longer could hold.

I make my own lists, in sentences and paragraphs rather than broken phrases, because language has not yet abandoned me. I am making such a list now, here in these pages. You've seen the long version. A short version of the story I've been telling you might say only:

Ruth, Earl, Dessa,

corn, crow, grass,

wind, dirt, sun.

Amos and James

Long before I held my own copy of the Good Book, a gift from
the queenly grandmother who wore feathered hats and drove a
white Cadillac, the Bible entered me from the air of my childhood as words spoken or sung. Sitting on the bare wooden
benches of Methodist churches, I heard ministers quote chapter
and verse in country accents, heard choirs chant psalms and
congregations bellow hymns, heard men in starched shirts and
women in cotton dresses read the Bible from pulpits as plain as
milking stools. At the supper table, head bowed, I heard snatches
of scripture offered in thanks for our fragrant food. Alone in bed,
on the brink of the dismaying darkness, I murmured every scrap
I could remember from God's word.

The word became not flesh but substance for me on my twelfth
birthday, when my mother's stepmother, paying a rare visit from
Chicago to our Ohio farm, climbed out of that creamy Cadillac
wearing a hat festooned with the downy feathers of quail, and
presented me with my first Bible. Zippered shut, bound in fake
black leather, no heavier than a meatloaf sandwich, it barely
filled my outspread hand. Yet when I tugged at the brass cross
that served as the zipper pull, and the book sprang open of its
own accord like a set of jaws, I found inside a thousand
whispery-thin pages containing everything that God had seen fit
to say, from the long-ago days when God still spoke in a clear
voice.

Now, forty birthdays later, the onionskin paper baffles my fingers and the minuscule print baffles my eyes. But at age twelve I set out to read the book from cover to cover, a few pages each night, not understanding half of what I read, yet pushing on, line by line, from "In the beginning" to the final "Amen." Although the title page informed me that I was reading the King James Version, "translated out of the original tongues," I had no idea whose tongues those were, nor who King James was, unless perhaps a kinsman of Solomon or David. I had no notion that this eerie language, with its *thee*'s and *thou*'s, had come down from the time of Shakespeare. I thought I was eavesdropping on God.

Every now and again I would pause in my nightly reading to gaze at the blank ceiling or the black window, the better to see the ancient stories. I supplied my own geography, using Lake Erie for the Red Sea, the Mahoning River for the Jordan, a sand and gravel pit for the desert, our wooded hills for the mountains of Israel, our garden for Gethsemane. I attributed my fears, my hopes, my hungers to the Biblical characters, and I gave them the faces of people I knew.

Amos, for example, that unwilling prophet, "an herdsman, and a gatherer of sycamore fruit," wore the gaunt face of an old farmer named John Sivy, a neighbor of ours, who spoke to me of dirt and crops and salvation while we forked silage into the troughs for his cows. When God uttered warnings through Amos, I heard Mr. Sivy's voice, earnest and gruff, sweetened by the lingering music of his native Swedish: "I will sift the house of Israel among all nations, like as *corn* is sifted in a sieve, yet shall not the least grain fall upon the earth." He was a thrifty man who built his own barns and kept the roofs tight and knew the difference between straight and crooked work, a man who could easily have said, "Behold, I will set a plumb line in the midst of my people Israel: I will not again pass by them any more." I took the sycamores of Amos to be the same as those that grew along the river bottom on Mr. Sivy's land, their white limbs writhing up through the darker branches of maples and oaks. I could not imagine why anybody would want to gather their fruits, those spiky balls that pricked my bare feet when I walked under the trees. But there were many puzzles in the Bible that I had trouble solving.

Amos, for example, strode through my imagination wearing Mr. Sivy's neatly patched overalls, but what did he mean by saying on the Lord's behalf that "a man and his father will go in unto the *same* maid, to profane my holy name"? The maid I understood to be one of those servants for rich folks, but I could not decipher the going in unto her. And what did Amos mean by saying "The virgin of Israel is fallen; she shall no more rise: she is forsaken upon her land; *there is* none to raise her up"? The only virgin I knew about was Mary the mother of Jesus, and I thought the label was part of her name, Virgin Mary, like the Babe in front of Ruth. For that matter, I could not make head nor tail of all those italics, which were scattered over the pages like a trail of bread crumbs that led nowhere: "And ye shall go out at the breaches, every *cow at that which is* before her; and ye shall cast *them* into the palace, saith the Lord." All I really caught hold of in a verse like that was the cow, and the slanty letters made even the cow seem mysterious.

The one italicized word that rang through loud and clear from the pages of Amos was *punishment*. It matched the one emotion that rang out from the hubbub of strange names and the litany of sins: God was angry. God was fed up. God was fit to be tied. God was going to make Israel pay for its wickedness: "Therefore thus saith the Lord; Thy wife shall be an harlot in the city, and thy sons and thy daughters shall fall by the sword, and thy land shall be divided by line; and thou shalt die in a polluted land: and Israel shall surely go into captivity forth of his land." Although puzzled by the harlot, the captivity, and the dividing line, I could still hear the terrible fury in this curse. Reading Amos was like listening through the closed door of my bedroom to my parents quarreling. The words were muffled, but the fierce feelings came through.

Why my parents fought is another story, and a long one, featuring too much booze and too little money. For this story, I can only say that their shouts and weeping drove me to scour the Bible at age twelve in search of healing secrets. I was also compelled to read those whispery pages by the onset of a desire I could not name and by the dread of death. The desire gathered in me like a charge of electricity, gathered and gathered until it arced out in a blaze of feeling so bright that I feared others must surely see it, sizzling toward a bush heavy with purple lilacs, toward a hammer gleaming in my father's hand, toward a snorting palomino ridden by a neighbor girl whose blond hair matched the horse's mane, above all toward the girl herself.

What was I supposed to do with this intense yearning? "Hate the evil, and love the good," Amos advised me. Fair enough— but how could I tell the one from the other? My body was an unreliable guide, with its craving eyes, itchy fingers, growling belly, and willful cock. In any case, my body was going to die. I had learned that with piercing certainty a few months before my grandmother gave me the Bible. While undergoing surgery, I suffered an ether nightmare that would stay with me for over ten years, until I was married and sharing a bed with someone whom I could lay my hand on in the dark. Although the surgery was minor, I nearly died from loss of blood. From the moment I came to, encircled by anxious faces in gauzy masks, I realized that I was temporary, a loose knot that would come untied.

Where could I hide from death? "Seek the Lord, and ye shall live," Amos told me, and Mr. Sivy told me the same. I sought the Lord passionately but also fearfully, because He was so often mad, waving his sword, calling down locusts and flood and fire. During my first journey through the Bible, the God of the Old Testament seemed to me like a peevish giant, hard to please and easily riled. If you were perfect, you might slide by unhurt. Otherwise, look out. This was the God who threw Adam and Eve out of the garden, sent Cain off into the wilderness, drowned almost everything that lived, kept Moses from setting foot in the Promised Land, turned Lot's wife to salt, sucked Jonah into the belly of a whale, buried Job under a blizzard of misery, slaughtered whole tribes, burned up cities, dried up crops, shook the foundations of the earth.

The Psalms were soothing, of course, and like anyone needing ointment for aches I returned to them over and over. But even the Psalms often sounded like cries from the bottom of a pit, as though the singers were pleading, Haul me up out of this misery, Lord! At the very end of his prophecy, Amos tossed out a few scraps of comfort, foreseeing a day when the people of Israel would be restored to their land, and the cities would be rebuilt, and the gardens would bear fruit, and the mountains would drip with wine. Yet those five hopeful verses were preceded by 139 menacing ones, and that seemed to me about the right proportion for this cantankerous God, who offered an ounce of mercy for a pound of pain.

My church taught me that the history of the Hebrews was a long preparation for the good news of Christ; I know better now, but as a boy I could read their history in no other light. While I crept through the tangles and terrors of the Old Testament, I knew that Jesus was coming, like the promise of spring after a hard winter. But I would not allow myself to skip ahead, so I was well along toward my thirteenth birthday before I reached the New Testament.

From the opening chapter of Matthew, I could sense a change in the divine weather. Storms would break out again later on, especially in the letters of Paul and the Revelation of John, with judgments as dark as any known to Amos or Jeremiah. Before voicing a single threat, however, Matthew told us about the gift of a miraculous baby, who entered the world bearing a name that meant "he shall save his people from their sins."

Although I could not have drawn up a list of my sins, I had no doubt that I needed saving. I suspected there was a flaw in me that caused my father to drink, my mother to fret, my older sister to be lonely, my younger brother to cry. Why else had I almost died from a simple operation? What else but some flaw in me could explain why I was gripped in nightmare by the whirlpool of oblivion? Why else did I wake with fists clenched and cock stiff and tears on my cheeks? What was wrong with me? Jesus would know. Jesus would see through me with his X-ray vision, find the crack in my soul, and mend it with a touch. To read on through the onionskin pages was to be laid bare before the gaze of Jesus; yet only in such nakedness was there hope of healing.

What I drew from that first reading of the New Testament is easier to recall if I pass over the weighty gospels and Paul's bewildering sermons, and if I speak instead about the letter of James, a book so brief that I could hold it all in my head at once. I figured the author was the same person who showed up on the title page of my zippered Bible as King James, and therefore his words must be of uncommon importance. Whoever this James might have been, he knew what I was up against. He knew about death: "For what is your life? It is even a vapour, that appeareth for a little time, and then vanisheth away." He knew how it felt to be split down the middle by doubt: "A double minded man is unstable in all his ways." He knew that a flaw in the soul can lead to family strife: "From whence come wars and fightings among you? come they not hence, even of your lusts that war in your members?"

Lust was the name, I decided, for those desires that gathered in me like electricity, the wild longings that blazed out from me toward lilac or horse or girl. Surely everyone close to me could hear the whine of a turbine in my belly, could see the flicker of sparks beneath my skin, could smell the scorching flesh. Women especially, with their penetrating eyes and delicate noses, would be sure to find me out.

During the visit when she gave me the zippered Bible, my grandmother took us for a drive in her white Cadillac, to show us how, at the push of a button, she could make the car rise on its springs, the better to negotiate our rutted country roads. She wore the quail hat, and it was all I could do to keep from reaching out of the backseat, where I sat with my sister and brother, and stroking those iridescent feathers.

Riding up front, my mother at one point mused aloud, "What on earth can we do about Scott's feet? They've begun to smell dreadfully."

My brother giggled and my sister stared at her lap.

"He should wash between his toes," Grandmother declared, lifting her voice so that I would be certain to hear. "With soap, mind you. Then rinse thoroughly and dry with a clean towel."

"Do you hear that?" Mother asked me sharply, for she had been giving me the same advice for months.

All during those months, I had been scrubbing and rinsing and drying until the skin between my toes was raw. Yet still by the end of each day my feet stank, and so did my armpits and crotch. It was as though a rebellion had broken out in the provinces of my body. James knew about this rebellion of the members, knew about simmering desire: "But every man is tempted, when he is drawn away of his own lust, and enticed. Then when lust hath conceived, it bringeth forth sin; and sin, when it is finished, bringeth forth death." That seemed to be my fate, laid out with the economy of a fortune in a Chinese cookie: You will be over-come by lust, fall into sin, and die. Was there any escape?

Well, James suggested, I could comfort orphans and widows. That was hard advice, because the widows on our back road scared me with their bent loneliness, and the only orphan nearby had been adopted by a carpenter's family, had been smothered in gifts, and finally ran off to California with a banjo player. Well, then, I could love my neighbors as myself. The trouble there was,

I had some ornery neighbors—folks who shot deer out of season from the windows of their trailers, wives who cheated on their husbands and husbands who beat their wives, kids who chewed tobacco and kicked their dogs—and besides, I could not very well love my neighbors as myself without first learning how to love myself.

Was there an easier way to save my soul? "If any man offend not in word," James assured me, "the same is a perfect man, and able also to bridle the whole body." I just might manage that. I could guard my tongue, never sass teachers or parents, never swear. When ugly words rose in me, I could seal my mouth and swallow them.

What else could I do? "If any of you lack wisdom," James wrote, "let him ask of God, that giveth to all men liberally, and upbraideth not; and it shall be given him." If there was one thing I lacked, it was wisdom, which I took to be the power to distinguish good from evil, and to choose the good. "Resist the devil," said James, "and he will flee from you. Draw nigh to God, and he will draw nigh to you. Cleanse your hands, ye sinners; and purify your hearts, ye double minded." I could more easily imagine drawing nigh to this God of the New Testament, who would not fly off the handle at the least little sin, than to the peevish giant of the Old Testament. I could risk praying to a God who was not armed to the teeth with floods and plagues and thunderbolts. Pray, then, said James, for "the prayer of faith shall save the sick, and the Lord shall raise him up; and if he have committed sins, they shall be forgiven him."

Here was the medicine for me. Here was the balm I drew from James, and more generally from the New Testament, the assurance that within me and beyond me, embracing my flawed, wavering, temporary self, there was an enduring and generous Power: "Every good gift and every perfect gift is from above, and cometh down from the Father of lights, with whom is no variableness, neither shadow of turning." Because my own life was shot through with darkness, I hungered for a God without shadow. Reading on beyond James, seeking a pound of mercy for my ounce of pain, I decided that Jesus had come to redeem not only us mortal sinners but also that old inscrutable tyrant.

Nine years passed before I read the Bible again from cover to cover, beginning on the first day of January 1967. By then I was twenty-one, a senior in college, a few months away from having to choose either jail or exile or Vietnam. If my first reading had been provoked by family turmoil, dread of death, and fear of my own rebellious body, my second reading was provoked by history. The personal drama of sin and salvation still played inside me, but it had been shoved onto a back stage by the public drama of civil rights marches, antiwar rallies, the burning of draft cards and bras, sit-ins at nuclear weapons factories, environmental protests, bombings on campuses, riots in the cities, body counts on the nightly news. How should I live my precious life in the face of so much confusion and suffering and need? What should I study? What work should I do? How should I answer when Uncle Sam called me to go fight in that wretched war? And where did that *should* come from?

Those were the questions that weighed on me as I trekked once more, line by line, from "In the beginning" to the final "Amen." For that second reading I put away my grandmother's Bible, which now seemed childish in its zippered jaws of fake black leather, quaint in its Jacobean English. Instead, I bought *The Oxford Annotated Bible*, a hefty volume that offered the Revised Standard Version in a padding of headnotes, footnotes, indices, historical surveys, and maps. The translation was more dependable, yet I could not help finding this modern English, stripped of *thee*'s and *thou*'s, to be rather bland by comparison with the version approved by King James. That the Bible was a translation, not a transcript of God's own speech, would have been news to me at age twelve. At twenty-one, I realized that the Bible was a ramshackle anthology, the work of many hands and centuries, bearing human stains on every page. By age twenty-one, I realized that God was not a bearded man in the sky, neither Lord nor Father, nothing that would fit inside the mind's frames, but instead the source and urge of everything.

During the nine years since my first reading, I had solved some Biblical puzzles. I had learned, for example, that the Middle Eastern sycamore was in fact the humble fig, not the gigantic tree with white branches gleaming along river banks in Ohio; so now I could understand why Amos gathered sycamore fruit. Although I had still not slept with a woman, I knew what it meant for a man and his father to go in unto the same maid, and I knew the distinction between virgin and harlot. I had figured out that when Amos railed against cows, he meant selfish women "who oppress the poor, who crush the needy," and not the harmless Holsteins I used to milk in Mr. Sivy's barn.

This time when I read Amos, I did not think of Mr. Sivy. I thought of Martin Luther King, Jr., with his prophet's voice so much louder and richer than the old Swedish farmer's, his face and body so much more expressive of holy anger. "Take away from me the noise of your songs," I could imagine Dr. King saying,

> *to the melody of your harps I will not listen.*
> *But let justice roll down like waters,*
> *and righteousness like an ever-flowing stream.*

When the God of Amos denounced Israel

> *because they sell the righteous for silver,*
> *and the needy for a pair of shoes—*
> *they that trample the head of the poor into the dust of the earth,*
> *and turn aside the way of the afflicted,*

I heard the resonant, grieving voice of Dr. King rising from the steps of the Lincoln Memorial or a dusty road in Mississippi or a jailhouse in Alabama.

Although I could locate on the maps in my Oxford Bible all the nations condemned by Amos, I was not interested in their ancient quarrels; the only country I brooded on was my own. The indictment of Israel sounded in my ears like a judgment on my wicked tribe:

> *Behold, I am setting a plumb line*
> *in the midst of my people America;*
> *I will never again pass by them;*
> *the high places of Washington shall be made desolate,*
> *and the sanctuaries of New York shall be laid waste,*
> *and I will rise against the house of Johnson with the sword.*

My own people seemed to me guilty of every sin catalogued by Amos: wars against the weak, neglect of the poor, sexual dalliance, drunkenness, empty religious ceremony, ostentatious wealth, taking of bribes, cheating in business, idolatry, injustice, greed. If the God of the prophets was still keeping track, there would be hell to pay for so much wickedness. The editors of the Revised Standard Version had gotten rid of all those bewildering italics, yet even without extra emphasis the word *punishment* still rang out from the pages of Amos like a furious refrain.

At age twenty-one I had not lost my fear of the grumpy tyrant, who vowed to slash, burn, enslave, and exile his unruly subjects. But I had come to recognize the tyrant as only one face of the Old Testament God, the image that a belligerent people would see when they looked in the mirror. Alongside the warrior chief, obsessed with rules and obedience, there was also the extravagant creator, raining equally on the just and the unjust, pouring forth the universe in grand indifference to our small doings. Amos knew this larger God, who

forms the mountains, and creates the wind,

and declares to man what is his thought;

who makes the morning darkness,

and treads on the heights of the earth.

In one magnificent passage, Amos caught both aspects of God, creator and destroyer:

He who made the Pleiades and Orion,

and turns deep darkness into the morning,

and darkens the day into night,

who calls for the waters of the sea,

and pours them out upon the surface of the earth,

the Lord is his name,

who makes destruction flash forth against the strong,

so that destruction comes upon the fortress.

So long as Amos was calling down destruction on neighboring countries, no one challenged him. But when he turned his sights on Israel and its king, the high priest Amaziah rebuked him. "O seer," said Amaziah, "go, flee away to the land of Judah, and eat bread there, and prophesy there; but never again prophesy at Bethel, for it is the king's sanctuary." Amos fired right back: "I am no prophet, nor a prophet's son; but I am a herdsman, and a dresser of sycamore trees, and the Lord took me from following the flock, and the Lord said to me, 'Go, prophesy to my people Israel.'"

When I read that exchange, I pictured Dr. King on the White House steps, preaching against the war in Vietnam, against the nuclear arms race, against racism and poverty and greed, against politicians and bosses who presided over so much cruelty and waste; then I pictured Dean Rusk or Robert McNamara or some other minion of President Johnson rushing outside to say, "Beat it, preacher, go deliver your message in some other country." Amos did not back down, and neither did Martin Luther King. A year after I graduated from college, Dr. King would be murdered in Memphis, the city of my birth. But in 1967 he still had a life to lose, and he kept risking that life by carrying the call for love into the precincts of hatred.

Would I have the courage to follow my own conscience when the summons arrived from my draft board? I knew that I could be trained to fight, and there were causes for which I would have fought, but I also knew that the killing of poor farmers in Vietnam was not such a cause. Behind the smoke and fog of politics, those farmers were defending their own land. Trying to imagine them, I recalled John Sivy pacing his fields. While I was away at college, those fields and the surrounding woods and much of my childhood ground had been flooded by a reservoir. Unlike the

Vietnamese, I could not blame a foreign invader for uprooting me, yet I could feel some twinge of their anger and pain. To be torn away from one's land, as Amos prophesied that the Israelites would be, seemed to me a terrible punishment, worse even than prison. If I said no to the war, however, and if the draft board refused to classify me as a conscientious objector, I would have to choose between exile and jail.

The further I read in the Bible that second time through, the more urgently I looked for passages to guide my choice. When I came to the Letter of James, for example, instead of worrying how to fool death or heal my family or save my soul, I focused on how he answered the question, "What causes wars, and what causes fightings among you?"

It was clear that James had in mind quarrels within the early Church, doctrinal struggles that would lead to schism after schism over the next two thousand years. Yet his reckoning seemed to apply equally well to the mayhem in Vietnam, the nuclear arms race, and the pitched battles in our cities: "What causes wars, and what causes fightings among you? Is it not your passions that are at war in your members? You desire and do not have; so you kill. And you covet and cannot obtain; so you fight and wage war." Reading those lines at age twenty-one, I concluded that the root of violence was not the longing to touch, for which I had felt so guilty at age twelve, but the longing to possess. Possess what? Power and prestige, said James, but above all wealth.

Like his master, Jesus, James was tough on the rich, because they took more than their share of the earth's bounty, because their luxury came out of the hides of the poor, and because they fancied their wealth would shield them against suffering and death. Think again, said James: "For the sun rises with its scorching heat and withers the grass; its flower falls, and its beauty perishes. So will the rich man fade away in the midst of his pursuits." When James called for us to "be doers of the word, and not hearers only," he took as his prime example service to the poor: "If a brother or sister is ill-clad and in lack of daily food, and one of you says to them, 'Go in peace, be warmed and filled,' without giving them the things needed for the body, what does it profit? So faith by itself, if it has no works, is dead."

To live our faith and not merely proclaim it, according to James, we should comfort the afflicted, befriend the lonely, house the homeless, speak the plain truth to all people, refrain from judging others, and never kowtow to the rich: "Has not God chosen those who are poor in the world to be rich in faith and heirs of the kingdom which he has promised to those who love him? But you have dishonored the poor man. Is it not the rich who oppress you, is it not they who drag you into court?"

Not long after I finished that second reading of the Bible, my draft board threatened to drag me into court, unless I agreed to wear a uniform and carry a gun. I refused. I wrote a letter explaining my reasons, quoting Amos and Jesus and James, quoting George Fox and Thoreau, Gandhi and Martin Luther King. I told the draft board I would mop floors in a mental hospital, tutor children in a ghetto, ladle out meals in a soup kitchen, but I would not help kill peasants in Vietnam. You will report for duty on the date we specify, the draft board answered. My conscience would not let me do that, I told them. Well, then, they replied, your conscience had better get ready for a showdown with a judge.

I did get ready. I underlined with red pencil every passage in *The Oxford Annotated Bible* that supported my pacifism, while ignoring those passages that seemed to justify war. Thus I skipped over the dire warnings in Amos, which sounded so much like the evening news:

> For behold, the Lord commands,
>
> and the great house shall be smitten into fragments,
>
> and the little house into bits.

And I skipped over those notorious words attributed to Jesus by Matthew: "Do not think that I have come to bring peace on earth; I have not come to bring peace, but a sword." Instead, I memorized the Sermon on the Mount. I rehearsed Paul's plea for a "ministry of reconciliation." I took to heart the assurance in James that "the wisdom from above is first pure, then peaceable, gentle, open to reason, full of mercy and good fruits, without uncertainty or insincerity."

Was I so utterly sincere? the judge might ask. Could I really set my conscience against my country? Were my beliefs so firm? I would confess that I had my doubts. Whereupon the judge might quote James against me, observing that "he who doubts is like a wave of the sea that is driven and tossed by the wind." Yes, I had bobbed on the waves of uncertainty. But if there was any truth to the claims Jesus made about God, I would tell the judge, then we were called to lay aside our weapons and love our enemies, for "the harvest of righteousness," according to James, "is sown in peace by those who make peace."

In the end, I never got the chance to deliver my scripture-laden speeches in court, because the draft board, no doubt weary of my pacifist letters, decided to shut me up. Instead of saying yea or nay to my request for conscientious objector status, they classified me 4-F, the category for those who, by reason of mental or physical defects, must not be drafted under any circumstances. My body was fit for war; only my dissident, Bible-haunted mind was amiss.

My mind is still haunted by the Bible. How many times have I read it through since preparing for my showdown with the judge? Maybe three times, maybe five; I have lost track. Although the cover is scuffed and the paper is jaundiced, I have stuck with my copy of the Oxford edition, if only because so many passages are underlined, first in red pencil, then in green and blue. When I open the book today—as a man married more than a quarter of a century, with two grown children—I still puzzle over death, over my father's drinking and my mother's grief, over sin and salvation; I still brood on war and cruelty and want.

But now in addition to those old concerns I also carry new ones. In James's tirades against the rich, I now hear an ecological indictment as well: "You have lived on the earth in luxury and in pleasure; you have fattened your hearts in a day of slaughter." In Amos's account of Judgment Day, I now see a foreshadowing of nuclear winter:

"And on that day," says the Lord God,
"I will make the sun go down at noon,
and darken the earth in broad daylight.
I will turn your feasts into mourning,
and all your songs into lamentation."

Here in the second half of life, I wonder less about my own small self, more about my species, my planet, and the universe. How have we come to be these divided creatures, split between thinking and wanting? How should we live? On what can we ground our moral judgments? Are they only masks for desire? Are they merely stratagems for fostering our genes? Are they cultural conventions, as flimsy as fashions in clothes? Do we have any direct access to the source of things? Or must we rely on those clumsy guides—scripture, history, popular opinion? What is the whole show about, if anything, and what is our role in it?

I no longer expect the Bible to yield definitive answers, to these or any other questions. Now I see this book as a record of one worthy tradition in the human search for knowledge, a search that seems to be our essential task. Now I think of God as the other side of the conversation that we have been carrying on with the universe since we learned to talk. Amos knew how we hunger for answers:

> "Behold, the days are coming," says the Lord God,
> "when I will send a famine on the land;
> not a famine of bread, nor a thirst for water,
> but of hearing the words of the Lord."

However scarce or abundant, the words of the Lord have never been clear. We have always had to contend with a power that speaks in whispers or thunder, in conundrums or codes. We raise our own voices to make up for the reticence of God. So Amos utters his prophecies; James composes his letter. Along with the many other witnesses in the Bible, they address an elusive One, who appears by turns as a tribal chief, an imperial judge, the Lord of all people, or the Creator of the cosmos.

I no longer have any use for the warrior or ruler or patriarch. I seek only the Creator, "who builds his upper chambers in the heavens," as Amos observed, *and founds his vault upon the earth;*

who calls for the waters of the sea,

and pours them out upon the surface of the earth.

From the surface of the earth we look outward and inward, seeking knowledge and more knowledge. "Of his own will he brought us forth by the word of truth," James insisted, "that we should be a kind of first fruits of his creatures." We are not first in time, of course, nor first in importance, but we seem to be first among the creatures in our potential for understanding. So far as we know, we are the only species capable of thinking about the universe as a whole. So far as we know, we alone are able to withdraw from the struggle for survival and the fever of reproduction long enough to gaze back at the source.

The quarrels that James lamented two thousand years ago are still splintering his Church; tribal hatred and warfare still grip Amos's neighborhood; the rich still squeeze their wealth out of the hides of the poor; the downtrodden still cry for justice. If you take the brief perspective of recorded history, we seem to be set in our deadly ways. But if you take the long perspective of human evolution, stretching over hundreds of thousands of years, then we appear as a young and fast-learning species. Generation by generation, with many backtracks and wrong turns, we are making ourselves at home in the universe. As our senses of smell, hearing, and vision have evolved in response to the world's odors and sounds and sights, as our scientific models have come to agree more and more exactly with the behavior of nature, so might our moral vision be developing slowly, haltingly, toward congruence with an order that is really *there,* independent of us, in the grain of things.

If Creation began as the great, undivided "I AM," then poured outward into space and time and myriad detail, perhaps we are the frontier of consciousness, the expanding self-awareness of the cosmos. If this is so, then human utterance, in all its forms, would be Creation's way of articulating and celebrating itself. James knew the risk and responsibility that comes with the power of speech. "And the tongue is a fire," he wrote. "With it we bless the Lord and Father, and with it we curse men, who are made in the likeness of God." Whether breathed into the air or inscribed on paper or broadcast into the depths of space, our words may curse or bless. The work of language deserves our greatest care, for the tongue's fire may devour the world, or may light the way.

Heartwood

From where I sit in the living room of this old American Four-square house that my wife and I have slowly fixed up, room by room, over twenty years, I can see half a dozen kinds of wood. There is the pale maple of a rocking chair, the black walnut of a sideboard, the poplar of baseboards and window trim, the yellow pine of wainscoting spangled with knots, the luster of a cherry bowl, and beneath it all the bold lines of a red oak floor. By walking through our small house, upstairs and down, I could find another handful of species—fragrant cedar, flamboyant sycamore and hickory, subtle white pine, elegant beech. In every case, we have sanded and stained and finished the wood so as to bring out the grain.

We preserve the grain for its beauty, for its grace, and also for a reminder of the living trees. Most of the wood in our house, in fact, comes from species that grow in the forests near our home here in southern Indiana. When sunlight draws my gaze across the gleaming floor, I think of oaks lifting their leaves toward the sky. When the maple rocker creaks beneath my weight, I remember gathering buckets of sap in the sugarbush. The lustrous cherry bowl recalls a mob of cedar waxwings stripping the fruit from a wild cherry tree. The smell of cedar in a closet reminds me of listening beside a grove of snow-covered cedars while a screech owl whinnied from dark tufted branches. Because I am surrounded by wood, even here indoors I never forget the great outside—the web of dirt and rain and sun and air on which all life depends.

I've loved tracing the grain in wood since childhood, when I helped my father build cupboards and tables, houses and barns. I learned to respect the grain when I sawed or chiseled a board, as if it were the stubborn character of the wood. Carpentry taught me how foolish it is to go against the grain, for you risk breaking your tool as well as spoiling your work. The straight grain in oak and pine will split if you don't take care, locust and elm are gnarled, and walnut will dull your blade. I learned to read the rings in trees cut across the grain, learned the uses of heartwood and sapwood, bird's-eye and burl. Working in my father's shop I learned to savor the sweet or sharp or fruity smell of sawdust, the perfume of the open air hidden in the depths of wood.

When my wife and I bought our house, more than twenty years ago, all the poplar trim was painted white. The paint did not stick well, for it had been applied over an original coating of shellac. On winter nights, as the boards contracted from the cold, white chips would flake off with a barely audible pop. We couldn't have our infant daughter crawling around and nibbling those flakes, so for our first remodeling job we scraped away that paint and refinished the poplar, bringing out its honeyed tone and its dark veins the color of butterscotch. Before, the trim had seemed cold and dead; after, it seemed alive and warm. Visitors to our house often run their hands along the door jambs or windowsills, as if stroking the flanks of a patient animal. Painting wood on the outside of a house may be necessary to protect it from weather, but painting wood inside a house seems like a betrayal of its wild past.

Trees breathe, my father taught me. They draw in what we cast off, carbon dioxide, and they give out what we crave, oxygen, and so our breath circles in and out of their pores. Only the outer husk of a tree is alive, the tender inch or two of sapwood just beneath the bark which carries vital juices between dirt and leaves. The inner core of the tree, the heartwood, is no longer living. It's not really dead, but merely still, finished, like a snapshot. Sliced open, the heartwood reveals a tree's history. So the grain exposed on our walls and floors and furnishings tells of fat years and thin, weather hard and mild, soils deep and shallow. The texture of each board is like the photograph of a face bearing the marks from a lifetime of blessings and blows.

Each plank in our floor is unique, and yet when the planks are laid side by side they resemble one another like brothers and sisters, faithful to the design of oaks. If the universe itself has a design, some deep and steadfast grain that reveals the kinship among all its parts, then what could be more important for a life's work than trying to discern that pattern? All of science is based on the faith that there is such a grain in things, at least in everything that can be measured. But what of those immeasurable things—feeling and thought, memory and longing, actions and words—is there a grain to them as well? Is there a pattern in our striving, a moral to be drawn from this history of breath?

Finding a logic in life is harder than finding order in the blinking of quasars or the dance of quarks. Nonetheless, I believe in such a logic. I believe there is a moral as well as a physical grain in things, and that our chief business is to discover what we can of that pattern and to align ourselves with it. Nature proves nothing about morality. And yet I cannot help feeling, as I gaze around at the quirky, lovely grain of wood in this old house, that to search for an underlying order, even in the mess of human affairs, is less foolish than to accept chaos as the only truth.

The root of the word *grain* means a kernel or seed, and that root in turn derives from an Indo-European word meaning to become ripe. The grain in the field, such as wheat or corn, and the grain in wood are akin, for they both reveal the earth's fertility. One sort of grain fills our bellies; the other shelters our bodies and links our minds to this great planetary home. We can see in the patterns of wood the swirls of cloud, the ripples in a creek, the tumult of a waterfall, the strata in rock, the tracings of creatures along a mud bank; we can see the branchings of our own veins; we can see the taut or tattered muscle of a heart. Wood grain speaks to us of wildness, the push of sap from roots into the tips of branches, the stress of wind, the struggle for a place in the sun. The same current of wildness flows through us, as we are reminded by surrounding ourselves with beautiful and patient wood.

Learning from the Prairie

In Salina, Kansas, first thing in the morning on the last day of October, not much is stirring except pickup trucks and rain. Pumpkins balanced on porch railings gleam in the streetlights. Scarecrows and skeletons loom in yards out front of low frame houses. Tonight the children of Salina will troop from door to door in costumes, begging candy. But this morning, only a few of their grandparents cruise the wet streets in search of breakfast.

In the diner where I come to rest, the average age of the customers is around seventy, and the talk is mainly about family, politics, and prices. Beef sells for less than the cost of raising it. There's a glut of soybeans and wheat. More local farmers have fallen sick from handling those blasted chemicals. More have gone bankrupt.

When a waitress in a leopard suit arrives to take an order from the booth next to mine, a portly man greets her by complaining that Halloween has turned out wet. "It's a true upset to me," the man says. "Last year I had two hundred children ring my bell." The waitress calls him honey and sympathizes.

An older woman bustles in from the street, tugs a scarf from her helmet of white curls, and declares to everyone in the diner, "Who says it can't rain in Kansas?"

At the counter, a woman wearing a sweatshirt emblazoned with three bears swivels around on her stool. "Oh, it rains every once in a while," she replies, "and when it does, look out!"

Here in the heart of Kansas, where tallgrass prairie gives way to midgrass, about twenty-nine inches of water fall every year, enough to keep the pastures thick and lure farmers into planting row-crops. Like farmers elsewhere, they spray pesticides and herbicides, spread artificial fertilizer, and irrigate in dry weather. They plow and plant and harvest using heavy machinery that runs on petroleum. They do everything the land-grant colleges and agribusinesses tell them to do, and still many of them go broke. And every year, from every plowed acre in Kansas, an average of two to eight tons of topsoil wash away. The streams near Salina carry rich dirt and troubling chemicals into the Missouri River, then to the Mississippi, and eventually to the Gulf of Mexico.

Industrial agriculture puts food on our tables and on the tables of much of the rest of the world. But the land and farmers pay a terrible price, and so do all the species that depend on the land, including us.

I've come to Salina to speak with a man who's seeking a radical remedy for all of that—literally radical, one that goes back to the roots, of plants and of agriculture. Over the past six or eight years I've bumped into Wes Jackson several times at gatherings of folks who worry about the earth's future, but this is my first visit to his home ground. Wes has been here since 1976, when he and his then-wife, Dana, founded the Land Institute, a place devoted to finding out how we can provide food, shelter, and energy without degrading the planet. He won a MacArthur fellowship in 1992 for his efforts, and he has begun to win support in the scientific community for a revolutionary approach to farming that he calls perennial polyculture—crops intermingled in a field that is never plowed, because the plants grow back on their own every year. The goal of this grand experiment is to create a form of agriculture that, like a prairie, runs entirely on sunlight and rain.

To reach the Land Institute, I drive past grain silos lined up in rows like the columns of a great cathedral; they are lit this early morning by security lights, their tops barely distinguishable from the murky sky. I drive past warehouses, truck stops, motels, fast-food emporiums, lots full of RVs and modular homes; past a clump of sunflowers blooming in a fence-corner at the turn-off for Wal-Mart; past filling stations where gas sells for eighty-five cents a gallon. The windshield wipers can't keep up with the rain.

When pavement gives way to gravel, I pass a feedlot where a hundred or so cattle stand in mud and lap grain from troughs. Since entering Kansas, I've seen billboards urging everyone to eat more beef, but the sight of these animals wallowing in a churned-up rectangle of mud does not stimulate my appetite. The feedlot is enclosed by electrified wire strung on crooked fence posts made from Osage orange trees. In a hedgerow nearby, living Osage oranges have begun to drop their yellow fruits, which are the size of grapefruits but with a bumpy surface like that of the human brain. After the road crosses the Smoky Hill River, it leaves the flat bottomland, where bright green shoots of alfalfa and winter wheat sprout from dirt the color of chocolate, then climbs up onto a rolling prairie, where the Land Institute occupies 370 acres.

Wes Jackson meets me in the yellow brick house that serves for an office. It's easy to believe he played football at Kansas Wesleyan, because he's a burly man, with a broad, outdoor face leathered by sun, and a full head of steel-gray hair. Although he'll soon be able to collect Social Security, he looks a decade younger. He wears a flannel shirt the shade of mulberries, blue jeans, and black leather boots that have quite a few miles on them. For a man who thinks we've been farming the wrong way for about 10,000 years, he laughs often and delights in much. He also talks readily and well, with a prairie drawl acquired while growing up on a farm in the Kansas River Valley, over near Topeka.

"I'm glad you found your way all right," he says. "Can't hide a thing out here on the prairie, but you'd be surprised at the people who get lost."

When I admit to having asked directions at a station that advertised gas for eighty-five cents a gallon, he tells me, "The price of gasoline is a symptom of our capacity for denial. We pay for gas based on how much of it is above ground, not how much is left below. We ignore its real scarcity."

Wes and I sit at the kitchen table while coffee perks, a copy machine on one side of us, a wood stove on the other. The walls are lined with shelves bearing jars full of seeds. Every now and again I ask a question, but mainly I listen. Wes talks in a voice as big as he is, all the while fixing me with a steady gaze through wire-rimmed spectacles, to make sure I'm following.

He points out that our whole economy rides on cheap oil, which he calls "fossil sunlight," and nowhere is this dependence more evident than in agriculture. Natural gas is the raw material for anhydrous ammonia, which farmers spread on fields to compensate for the loss of natural fertility. We hammer the soil, he says, then put it on life support. We replace draft horses and hand labor with diesel-powered machines. We replace the small-scale farming of mixed crops with vast plantations of single crops, usually hybrids, which are so poorly adapted that we have to protect them from weeds and pests with heavy doses of petroleum-based poisons.

While cheap oil has accelerated our journey down the wrong path, we set out on that path long before we discovered the convenience of fossil sunlight, according to Wes. Our ancestors made the key mistake at the very beginnings of agriculture, when they started digging up the fields and baring the soil. The great river civilizations along the Tigris, Euphrates, Ganges, and Nile could get away with that for a while, since floods kept bringing in fresh dirt. But as populations expanded and tillage crept out of the river bottoms into the hills, the soil began to wash away.

"The neolithic farmers began mining ecological capital," he explains. "That was the true Fall, worse than anything poor Eve might have done."

Wes knows his Bible, and he draws from history and philosophy and literature as easily as from plant genetics, the field in which he earned his Ph.D. at North Carolina State. At one point he quotes a famous phrase from the prophet Isaiah, then questions whether we're actually better off beating swords into plowshares. Wes is wary of swords, but also wary of plows. Where our ancestors went wrong, he believes, was in choosing to cultivate annual crops, which have to be planted each year in newly turned soil. The choice is understandable, since annual plants take hold more quickly and bear more abundantly than perennials do, and our ancestors had no way of measuring the long-term consequences of all that digging and tilling.

But what's the alternative? How else can we feed ourselves?

Wes takes me outside to look at the radically different model for agriculture that he's been studying for more than twenty years—the native prairie. Because the rain hasn't let up, we drive a short distance along the road in his battered Toyota pickup, then pass through a gate and go jouncing onto an eighty-acre stretch of prairie that's never been plowed. The rusty, swaying stalks of big bluestem wave higher than the windshield. The shorter stalks of little bluestem, Indian grass, and switchgrass brush against the fenders. We stop on the highest ridge and roll down the windows so rain blows on our faces, and we gaze across a rippling, sensuous landscape, all rounded flanks and shadowy crevices.

"This would be a fine spot for the Second Coming," Wes murmurs. After a pause he adds, "Not that we need saving here in Kansas."

The grasses are like a luxurious covering of fur, tinted copper and silver and gold. In spring or summer this place would be fiercely green and spangled with flowers, vibrant with butterflies and songbirds. Now, in the fall, Wes reports, it's thick with pheasant, quail, and wild turkey. He and his colleagues don't harvest seeds here, but they do burn the prairie once every two or three years, and they keep it grazed with Texas longhorns, whose bellows we can hear now and again over the purr of engine and rain. Eventually the cattle will give way to bison, a species better adapted to these grasslands. From the pickup, we can see a few bison browsing on a neighbor's land, their shaggy coats dark with rain.

In every season the prairie is lovely beyond words. It supports a wealth of wildlife, resists diseases and pests, holds water, recycles fibers, fixes nitrogen, builds soil. And it achieves all of that while using only sunlight, air, snow, and rain. If we hope to achieve as much in our agriculture, Wes argues, then we'd better study how the prairie works. Not just the Kansas prairie, but every one we know about elsewhere, works by combining four basic types of perennial plants—warm-season grasses, cool-season grasses, legumes, and sunflowers—all growing back year after year from the roots. The soil is never laid bare. The prairie survives droughts and floods and insects and pathogens because the long winnowing process of evolution has adapted the plant communities to local conditions.

"The earth is an ecological mosaic," Wes explains. "We're only beginning to recognize the powers inherent in local adaptation."

If you wish to draw on that natural wisdom in agriculture, he tells me as we drive toward the greenhouse, then here in Kansas you need to mimic the structure of the prairie. It's all the more crucial a model, he figures, because at least 70 percent of the calories that humans eat come directly or indirectly from grains, and all our grains started as wild grasses. For nearly a quarter-century, Wes and his colleagues have been working to develop what he calls perennial polyculture—as opposed to the annual monoculture of traditional farming—by experimenting with mixtures of wild plants. Recently they've focused on Illinois bundleflower, a nitrogen-fixing legume whose seed is about 38 percent protein; *Leymus,* a mammoth wild rye; eastern gama grass, a bunchgrass that's related to corn but is three times as rich in protein; and Maximilian sunflower, a plentiful source of oil.

In the sweet-smelling greenhouse, we find seeds from these and other plants drying in paper bags clipped to lines with clothes pins. The bags are marked so as to identify the plots outside where the seeds were gathered; each plot represents a distinct ecological community. Over the years, researchers at the Land Institute have experimented with hundreds of combinations, seeking to answer four fundamental questions, which Wes recites for me in a near-shout as rain hammers down on the greenhouse roof: Can perennial grains, which invest so much in roots, also produce high yields of seed? Can perennial species yield more when planted in combination with other species, as on the prairie, than when planted alone? Can a perennial polyculture meet its own needs for nitrogen? Can it adequately manage weeds and insects and disease?

So far, Wes believes, they can answer a tentative yes to all those questions. For example, his daughter Laura, now a professor of biology at the University of Northern Iowa, has identified a mutant strain of eastern gama grass whose seed production is four times greater than normal—without any corresponding loss of root mass or vigor.

More and more scientists are now testing this approach. After returning home from Salina, I'll contact Stephen Jones at Washington State University, a plant geneticist who is developing perennial forms of wheat suited to the dry soils of his region. I'll correspond with a colleague of Jones's at Washington State, John Reganold, a professor of soil science who predicts that with these design-by-nature methods, "soil quality will significantly improve—better structure, more organic matter, increased biological activity, and thicker topsoil." I'll learn about efforts in the Philippines to develop perennial forms of rice. I'll speak with the director of the plant-biotechnology program at the University of

Georgia, Andrew Paterson, who is also experimenting with perennial grains. I'll contact Stuart Pimm at the University of Tennessee, a conservation biologist who has reported in the journal *Nature* on Land Institute experiments that show that mixtures of wild plants not only rival monocultures in productivity but also inhibit weeds and resist pathogens while building fertility.

I'll contact all those people, and more, after returning home from Salina. But right now I'm listening to the fervent voice of Wes Jackson, who's lamenting that the United States loses 2 billion tons of topsoil a year to erosion. The cost of that—in pollution of waterways, silting of reservoirs, and lost productivity—is $40 billion, according to the U.S. Department of Agriculture. Wes estimates that only 50 million of the 400 million tillable acres in the United States are flatland, and even those are susceptible to erosion. The remaining 350 million acres—seven-eighths of the total—range from mildly to highly erodible, and thus are prime territory for perennial polyculture.

He flings these statistics at me as we drive into Salina for lunch at a Mexican restaurant. Maybe what set him hungering for Mexican food were the strings of bright red jalapeño peppers hanging in the greenhouse among the brown paper sacks full of seeds. Whatever the inspiration, Wes launches into his plateful of burritos with the zeal of a man who has done a hard morning's work. As we eat, a nearby television broadcasts a game between Kansas State and the University of Kansas. Checking the score, Wes explains, "My nephew plays for KU at guard, my old position." When he learns that Kansas is losing, he turns his back to the TV and resumes telling me about what he calls natural-systems agriculture.

"The old paradigm," he says, "is the industrial model, which figures we can beat nature, make it dance to our tune, use up whatever we need and dump our wastes wherever's convenient. The new paradigm, the one we're following at the Land, believes less in human cleverness and more in natural wisdom. The prairie knows what it's doing—it's been trying things out for a long while—and so we've made ourselves students of the prairie."

Transforming perennial polyculture from a research program into a feasible alternative for the working farmer will require many more years of painstaking effort, Wes admits. Researchers must breed high-yielding varieties of perennial grains and discover combinations of species that rival the productivity of the wild prairie. Engineers must design machinery for harvesting mixed grains that may ripen at different times. Farmers must be persuaded to try the new seeds and new practices, and consumers must be persuaded to eat unfamiliar foods.

In keeping with his mission, before we leave the Mexican restaurant Wes urges me to try the whole wheat tortilla chips. "They're a lot tastier than the cornmeal, don't you think?"

I try them, and I agree.

It's still raining when we climb back into the pickup, and as we drive into the countryside Wes keeps shaking his head at the black slurry pouring off the fields. "That's gold running away," he says. "Farmers are always worrying about money, and right there's pure wealth just washing away. It takes up to a thousand years to make an inch of topsoil."

He goes on to speak about the need for training farmers, a subject close to his heart. "The children in rural schools are one day going to be in charge of the 400 million acres of tillable land in this country. So they'll have the greatest ecological impact of any group." To help inform those schools—and help resettle the small towns in which many of those children will grow up—the Land Institute has created a Rural Community Studies Center in Matfield Green, a tiny settlement in the Flint Hills about a hundred miles southeast of Salina. "We want to bring the message of ecology to bear on the curriculum of rural schools," he says. "I want those young people to go to Kansas State, Ohio State, all the ag schools, and ask questions that push beyond the existing paradigm."

How well would annual monoculture perform if it weren't subsidized by inputs of petroleum and groundwater, and if it weren't allowed to write off the ecological costs of pesticides and herbicides and erosion? To answer that question, the Land Institute has devoted 150 acres to the Sunshine Farm, a ten-year project for growing livestock and conventional crops without fossil fuels, chemicals, or irrigation. The Sunshine Farm is where we go next, and the arrival of our truck wakes three dappled-gray Percheron draft horses from their rainy drowse in a paddock beside the barn. For the heaviest work there's also a tractor, but it shelters inside the barn and it runs on bio-diesel fuel made from soybeans and sunflower seeds. The farmhouse is heated with wood, and all the buildings are lit from batteries charged by a bank of photovoltaic cells.

Six years into the study, data from the Sunshine Farm are providing a truer measure of how much conventional farming costs. Marty Bender, who manages the farm, explains, "We look at the energy content of all the crops and livestock that we produce, and we look at the inputs—fuels, feeds, stock, seeds, tools, labor. If you divide our outputs by our inputs, the ratio is comparable to what you see on Amish farms. And that tells me we're on the right track."

"When all the numbers are in," Wes predicts, "I'm sure the prairie's way will beat the pants off the industrial way."

Back in the yellow-brick office, Wes unrolls onto a table what he calls the Big Chart, which lays out a twenty-five-year research plan. The boxes on the chart frame problems to be solved, and the arrows all point toward the vision of a sustainable agriculture that will overturn the mistaken practices of the past ten millennia. It's a bold scheme. Already, scientists like Stephen Jones, Andrew Paterson, John Reganold, and Laura Jackson have begun to work on pieces of the puzzle. With half a dozen full-time investigators and their assistants, plus eight student interns and five or six graduate students each year, the Land Institute operates now with an annual budget of $850,000, supported by foundations and private donors and the tireless labor of many friends.

This endeavor, now almost a quarter-century old, nearly died in infancy. As a young man with a family, Wes gave up a tenured position at California State in order to homestead in Kansas, then put every cent he had into starting the Land Institute. "Six months later," he recalls, "our only building burnt down, with all our books and tools. A great darkness came over me. It seemed like the world was telling me to quit. But if you're raised on a farm you're used to making things work. If you don't get it right the first time, you have another go at it. So we rebuilt."

To carry on the necessary future research, Wes calculates

they'll need between $5 million and $7 million a year—not much money when you consider that estimated yearly loss of $40 billion from soil erosion in the United States. This higher level of funding can only come with backing from the U.S. Department of Agriculture and even from agribusiness firms. "So far," he admits, "we've hit a brick wall at USDA. When you talk with them about learning from the prairie, following nature as measure and pattern, their eyes glaze over."

He realizes how difficult it will be to pry money from institutions whose philosophy of farming he so squarely opposes, but he relishes the challenge. "In America," he tells me as I prepare to leave, "we've got mostly two kinds of scientists—the ones who get us in trouble, and the ones who tell us what the troubles are—but very few who are looking for solutions. Here at the Land Institute, we're looking for solutions."

Before I go, I can't help asking him to explain how a Kansas farm boy grew up to become a visionary who's trying to revolutionize farming. He can't say for sure. His family's been in Kansas since 1854 (the year that *Walden* was published). His great-grandfather fought alongside John Brown at the Battle of Blackjack Creek, against proslavery hooligans from Missouri. His grandchildren are the sixth generation to live in the state. So he feels committed to this region for the long haul, and he wants it to be a beautiful and fertile place well after he's gone. "It seems like, no matter what else I tried, I just kept thinking about the source—soil, water, photosynthesis, the things that sustain us." Is he hopeful that a durable form of agriculture will be found in time to feed the earth's swelling population? "We don't know how this is all going to turn out," he admits. "But the risky thing is to do nothing, to keep on going the way we've been going. No matter how dark the times, it's still worthwhile to do good work."

The next morning, as I drive east through even heavier rain toward my home in Indiana, the radio carries reports of brimming rivers and flooded roads across Kansas. The plowed fields I pass are gouged by rivulets and the roadside ditches run black with dirt. But where grass covers the land, there's no sign of runoff, for the prairie keeps doing what it's learned how to do over thousands of years—holding water, building soil, waiting for spring.

Cabin Dreams

If you live in a small house and love reading, as I do, eventually you will cover every bare wall with shelves and every shelf with books. My house passed the saturation point some years ago, so that now, for each new volume admitted through the front door, an old one must be ushered out the back. The exiled books usually fall from grace in stages. Newcomers join the unread volumes on my bedside table, and when that pile begins tottering, I survey the lot and demote a few to the bedroom shelves, and from those groaning shelves I then demote other books to the study, then others in turn to the front room, the dining room, the basement, and finally out into the cold.

I feel guilty enough over banishing these books without selling them as well, so I donate them to the Salvation Army, the Red Cross, or the county library, or I match them up with my friends, or I give them to students who seem to need what these covers hold. No matter what precautions I take to find worthy homes, however, I still feel that every exiled book is a piece of my past, a piece of *me,* cast out forever and ever.

Since the winnowing is so painful, and since I can afford more space, why don't I build a library wing onto this cramped house? Or why don't I move into a bigger one? Let me answer those questions by referring you to the shelves beside my bed, for there, among the volumes that have survived repeated winnowings, clinging in place for years, sometimes for decades, you will find book after book by meditative souls who dwelt contentedly in cabins.

There is *The Outermost House,* for example, Henry Beston's account of a year he spent in a two-room cottage on the outer beach of Cape Cod, watching "the flux and reflux of ocean, the incomings of waves, the gatherings of birds, the pilgrimages of the peoples of the sea, winter and storm, the splendour of autumn and the holiness of spring." Or there is Wendell Berry's *The Long-Legged House,* with its title essay about a fishing camp raised on stilts beside the Kentucky River, where, as a teenager, Berry first recognized "the possibility of a greater, more substantial peace—a decent, open, generous relation between a man's life and the world," and where he later brought his wife for the first summer of their marriage, and where he began the writing that would root him ever more deeply in his home ground.

And there are collections of letters and meditations by Thomas Merton, who lived during his last years in a concrete-block hermitage, much of the time without electricity or indoor plumbing, on the grounds of a Trappist monastery not far from Berry's Kentucky farm. "All I can say about the life in the cottage," Merton wrote in *The Hidden Ground of Love,* "is that it makes immense sense, and does not necessarily imply any kind of serious break with reality: quite the contrary, I am back in touch with it."

Getting in touch with reality has been a prime motive for all the cabin-dwellers whose books hold their position so stubbornly on my bedroom shelves. Aldo Leopold roved out from his shack on a battered Wisconsin farm to watch the sky-dance of woodcocks, to savor the blooming of prairie flowers, to hear

Canada geese honking by on their migrations, to measure the growth of white pines, to notice all the enduring patterns he records so exuberantly in *A Sand County Almanac*. Edward Abbey tells in *Desert Solitaire* about living for three years in a dumpy house trailer while he worked as a park ranger in Arches National Monument, just outside of Moab, Utah. The trailer was so small, so clearly an alien box in this primal country of sand and rock, that he took every opportunity of going outside. To shelter from the blistering sun and the occasional rain, he rigged up an awning in the open air, and there he cooked his meals over fires of juniper wood and slept with his face stroked by wind.

Sue Hubbell made her home in a cabin in the Ozark Mountains while writing the chronicle of life and love and land called *A Country Year,* with its fetching subtitle borrowed from Rilke, *Living the Questions.* After a numbing divorce, Hubbell kept a roof over her head by selling honey. Then one afternoon, while her bees were gathering pollen from wild cherry blossoms, she paused in a sunbeam to watch them: "The world appeared to have been running along quite nicely without my even noticing it. Quietly, gratefully, I discovered that a part of me that had been off somewhere nursing grief and pain had returned."

The first cabin Harlan Hubbard shared with his wife, Anna, was a floating one. In *Shantyboat,* he reports how they drifted down the Ohio River, then tied up for days or months at a time, then drifted again, on down the Mississippi into the bayou country of Louisiana. When the time came to settle, they chose one of their favorite mooring sites along the Ohio, a secluded spot far from cities, and there they built a house as small and tidy as the shantyboat. These experiments in simplicity, Hubbard wrote in

Payne Hollow, "gave a direction to our lives that Anna had never before contemplated; for me it was the fulfillment of old long-ings; yet we were both led on by a common desire to get down to earth and to express ourselves by creating a setting for our life together which would be in harmony with the landscape."

I know those old longings. For as long as I can remember, I've yearned to get down to earth, to dwell in harmony with the land, to live so simply that I never lose sight of the great world beyond the walls of my house. The most durable of my books remind me of that primary world, the one that embraces and outlives every-thing humans have made. Thus I keep on the shelves beside my bed volumes of poetry by Robinson Jeffers and William Butler Yeats, each of whom lived in a small stone tower—in the case of Jeffers, one that he built himself. "If you should look for this place after a handful of lifetimes," Jeffers wrote in "Tor House,"

> *Look for foundations of sea-worn granite, my fingers had the art*
> *To make stone love stone, you will find some remnant.*

The retreat where Yeats brooded on love and war and Irish lore was Thoor Ballylee, which appears in poem after poem:

> *A winding stair, a chamber arched with stone,*
> *A grey stone fireplace with an open hearth,*
> *A candle and a written page.*

In *Memories, Dreams, Reflections,* another of my bedside books, I can read how Carl Jung built a tower of stone as a place for retreat and meditation on the shore of Lake Zurich. He cut the stones in the nearby quarries of Bollingen, laid the foundations in a circle, and raised the walls slowly, taking care over the place-ment of each block. He meant for the dwelling to be primitive, more like a cave than a house, so he left out the modern conveniences, such as electricity and running water. Leaving his busy practice of therapy in the city, where he labored to cure the psychological ills of other people, Jung withdrew to this stone hut in order to restore his own spirit: "From the beginning I felt the Tower as in some way a place of maturation—a maternal womb or a maternal figure in which I could become what I was, what I am and will be. It gave me a feeling as if I were being reborn in stone."

The dwellings described in *Black Elk Speaks,* another of the books I've kept close by me for years, were made of buffalo hides and cottonwood poles, but they were also round, like Jung's tower, and for the same reason: as a reminder of how nature works. "The life of a man is a circle from childhood to childhood," Black Elk explains, "and so it is in everything where power moves. Our tepees were round like the nests of birds, and these were always set in a circle, the nation's hoop, a nest of many nests, where the Great Spirit meant for us to hatch our children."

Even when they do not name the mystery at the heart of things, these writers who've chosen simple dwellings seem more than usually attentive to the way the spirit moves. In *The Narrow Road to the Deep North,* and in other of his travel sketches, the Japanese poet Matsuo Bashō tells of staying in a series of small retreat houses built by his disciples, listening to crickets, touching the moss, watching the moon, hoping to sense the current flowing in the heart of things. In *Pilgrim at Tinker Creek,* Annie Dillard compares her house in Virginia's Blue Ridge Mountains to a hermitage, an "anchor-hold," whence she could wander out "to explore the neighborhood, view the landscape, to discover at least *where* it is that we have been so startlingly set down, if we can't learn why." On her walks, she often visited an even smaller house, a tumbledown cottage in a nearby meadow: "It was a one-room cottage; you could manage (I've thought this through again and again—building more spartan mansions, o my soul) a cot, a plank window-desk, a chair (two for company, as the man says), and some narrow shelves."

The man whispering in Dillard's head is that notorious advocate of the simple life, Henry David Thoreau, who wrote of his own experiment in *Walden:* "I had three chairs in my house; one for solitude, two for friendship, three for society." Built out of recycled lumber from an Irishman's shanty and of white pines cut down from Ralph Waldo Emerson's woodlot, that house was famously small, ten feet by fifteen, and so sparsely furnished that Thoreau could set everything out in the yard when he wished to sweep the floor. Among those scant possessions were books, which he regarded as necessities ranking close behind food and clothing and shelter. Not just any books, of course, but the vital and durable ones, "the oldest and the best, [which] stand naturally and rightfully on the shelves of every cottage," for they offer "words addressed to our condition exactly."

The books that stand on my own shelves years after year, while hundreds of others go into exile, are those, like *Walden,* that speak to my condition, that help me pay attention to the inward and outward realities, that guide me toward a meaningful life. Why open any book, after all, if the reading does not return us to the world with a richer sense of who and where we are?

Wood Work

After nearly thirty years of living in town and hankering for the country, my wife and I bought a few acres of land bordering a state forest in southern Indiana, six miles from our front door, with visions of camping out there on weekends among the hawks and creeks and deer. The only attraction on the land not put there by nature was the shell of a building that we thought we might fix up into a cabin. The previous owners had raised the frame of two-by-fours on a concrete slab, roofed it over, and covered the outside with loosely nailed planks, before running out of money, or patience, or both. By the time we bought the place, the shingles and planks had begun to curl, wasps had built nests under the eaves, and spiders had claimed every corner. Still, Ruth and I saw possibilities in that forsaken shell. We didn't want anything fancy, just a place where we could rest our legs and take refuge from foul weather, with lights and water and heat and a view of the woods.

I fooled myself into thinking I could fix up the cabin myself, as if I were still twenty-five years old with a beginner's job and energy to burn. I looked forward to sawing and hammering, wiring and plumbing. But I was fifty when we bought the place, devoured by my job, short on energy and time. Two years passed. Ruth and I barely managed to clean out the shell, without making a start on renovation. So it was clear that we would have to hire carpenters if the job was ever going to get done, and it was equally clear that we should hire the two men who had done fine work for us at our house in town, Deryl Dale and Steve Neuenschwander. Deryl writes songs and reads books for recreation, while Steve favors hang gliding and rock climbing, but when they're on the job, both men apply themselves to wood or drywall or tile with rare intelligence and skill.

They started on the cabin this past October, while maples on the ridge out back glowed scarlet and laggard geese honked across the sky heading south. It's now late January; our part of Indiana is thawing from a siege of ice, and just yesterday I saw my first geese of the season beating their way north. For the past four months I've gone out to the cabin every spare moment, to deliver materials, discuss plans, heft a hammer or a paint brush, or simply to watch Deryl and Steve work. I watch them as one who admires any work carried out with devotion and craft, but also as one who dreamed for a spell in childhood of becoming a carpenter.

Early in his marriage my father built furniture for a living, mainly chairs and beds—because everybody likes to sit down, he told me, and everybody has to sleep. Then after Hitler's war put an end to that job, he kept a wood shop in the basement or garage of every house he lived in for the rest of his days. While I was growing up I spent hundreds of hours with him in one or another of those cluttered shops, learning the use of tools, breathing sawdust. I listened to him sing snatches of old songs, and I picked up dozens of the sayings that he muttered, like incantations, over wood: "Were you born that way, or did you just grow crooked?"

"Come on, now, you were cut to fit there, and you know it."
" 'Let me see,' said the blind man—and he picked up his hammer and saw."

Time and again I watched my father turn piles of lumber into
tables, closets, jewelry boxes, stools. When I learned in Sunday
school that Jesus was a carpenter, like his father, Joseph, I
thought I understood at least this much about those long-ago,
mysterious figures out of the Bible: understood how their ears
rang from the hammering, how their eyes watered from the dust,
how their fingers gripped the worn handles, how they rejoiced in
making something useful out of wood. As an apprentice to my
father, I worked my way up from sweeping the floor to whittling
toy boats, from turning walnut bowls on a lathe to cobbling together doghouses out of scrap.

One summer during high school I got my first chance to help
build real houses when a local contractor hired me for his crew.
At first I dug trenches for footers, mixed mortar, carried lumber
for other people to cut and nail. In the evenings I lay down with
the weight of stubborn matter aching in my bones. Over the
course of that summer the contractor taught me how to imagine
every step from a hole in the ground to a finished house, and he
began teaching me how to build what I had imagined. To finish
those lessons in carpentry would have taken far more than a summer. By August I had learned enough to lay out a wall of studs
and plates, to plumb a window or shingle a roof. Years later I
would need every bit of that knowledge to help finish the house
in which my parents retired; I would need it to restore the run-
down house that Ruth and I bought in town, and then to repair the
house my mother bought near us after my father died; and I need

that knowledge now to help Deryl and Steve turn the empty husk of a building on our land into a cabin full of grace and light.

The lineman from Public Service Indiana who came out to hook up our electrical service at the cabin was pushing sixty, paunchy, wearing bib overalls and a baseball cap. He tugged on the bill of that cap in response to my hello, then he climbed into the bright yellow bucket of the power lift on the back of his truck and hoisted himself up toward the dangling wires at the top of our utility pole. I couldn't see any transformer nearby, so I asked him where he would shut off the power before starting work.

"I don't shut it off," he called down to me. "I work on it hot, but respectful, like it was a snake that could bite."

He tugged on heavy rubber gloves, then began wrestling those thick, stubborn, highly charged wires. They might really have been snakes, for all the care he took in handling them. He'd been doing this for thirty years or more, but that didn't make him hasty. He took his time, made sure of every move, and performed this dangerous work without a hitch.

While I never became a carpenter, I learned a great deal about the meaning of good work from building houses and helping my father in his shop, and I carried those lessons with me into the trade I did eventually take up, that of writing. I came to believe that a writer, like a carpenter, ought to make useful and durable things, with a respect for materials and craft, and with an eye for beauty. As in carpentry, so in writing one ought to make tight joints and clean lines, avoiding showy ornaments and cheap tricks. No matter how polished the surface of your work, there ought to be substance underneath. What you build ought to last, bearing up under rough weather and the abrasion of time. You ought to give to the work the best you have, without holding back, and the work ought to give you, in turn, the pleasure of exercising your full strength and knowledge and skill.

Although carpenters often build dwelling places for strangers, and writers make books for people they will never meet, both writing and building are more satisfying if you know, or at least imagine, those who will inhabit your house or your book. Deryl and Steve always practice their art for owners with whom they can talk. With Ruth and me, they talk about everything from the roofline of the cabin to the baseboard trim. Do we want a porch out front so we can sit and watch the meadow bloom? Shouldn't we side the cabin with cedar rather than vinyl, so it will blend into the forest? Where should we put the wood stove? Oak or maple for the floor? How high the bookshelves? How wide the doors? And so, by talking and listening, Deryl and Steve bear in mind the people who will use their handiwork. In the same way, I bear in mind an audience as I write—I think of my family and neighbors and friends, I think of my students, I think of people whom I've met on my travels, I think of writers living and dead whose books have nourished me. They are my cloud of witnesses. Hoping that the words I lay down will speak to them, I write with a feeling of responsibility and love.

When I consider what makes any work satisfying, I'm guided by the example of carpentry as much as by that of writing. If work is going to fill our souls and not merely our bank accounts, then it should serve a real human need. It should offer nourishment or shelter, for example, offer knowledge or consolation, instead of gimmicks or gadgets or sops for our vanity. Good work leaves the world enriched and not diminished. It honors raw materials—wood or words, petroleum or steel—by using them sparingly and honestly. It permits us to imagine the whole of a task, from beginning to end, and then to carry it through, either alone or in cooperation with others. By inviting us to give ourselves entirely to the task, it relieves us for a time from egotism and greed. Good work allows us to express our beliefs as well as our talents, and thus to play our small part in sustaining the Creation.

I don't claim always to fulfill those ideals in my own work, only to aim at them. That's what ideals are for, after all—to give us targets for our labors and longings. The word in the Greek New Testament most often translated as *sin* is *hamartia,* which means to miss the target, as when an arrow flies astray. Of course one may practice any trade in a slapdash way. I've met my share of lazy carpenters and sleazy writers, who care only about making an easy buck. But at least in building houses and books there is always the *possibility* of finding meaning in your work. The same cannot be said about many jobs in factories and offices, jobs that end in shoddy goods, squander the earth's bounty, break the back or spirit of the worker. If you defend tobacco companies from lawsuits, or spot-weld fenders on gas-guzzling cars, or shuffle papers in a business devoted to trivial pursuits, or design advertisements for junk, or gamble on the securities market with other people's money, or cut down old-growth timber for pulp, or haul useless merchandise from town to town, you may lie down at night and wonder whether you've done the earth more harm than good that day.

If you seek liberation, according to the Buddha, then you must practice right livelihood. The Shaker visionary, Mother Ann Lee, put the same advice in a memorable phrase: "Hands to work, hearts to God." Dorothy Day called on those who joined her in the Catholic Worker movement to act out through their labor the gospel injunctions—love your neighbors, feed the hungry, house the homeless, comfort the suffering. How you provide the necessities of life, for yourself and for those who depend on you, is a spiritual matter. It is as important to earn your livelihood in a worthy manner as it is to meditate or pray. In fact, right livelihood is a kind of prayer, a way of acknowledging our gifts and sharing our talents.

The advice that we should make of our work a spiritual act might seem to be at odds with God's famous curse in the book of Genesis. For having eaten of the forbidden fruit, God tells Adam,

> *"Cursed is the ground because of you;*
> *in toil you shall eat of it all the days of your life;*
> *thorns and thistles it shall bring forth to you;*
> *and you shall eat the plants of the field.*
> *In the sweat of your face*
> *you shall eat bread*
> *till you return to the ground,*
> *for out of it you were taken;*
> *you are dust,*
> *and to dust you shall return."*

But notice that God curses the soil, not the labor. Work does indeed become toil when the ground is cursed—when the conditions in which we labor are grudging or bleak, when there is no joy in the effort, no hope. Those are the conditions often faced by the poor, in our own slums and trailer parks, and in entire nations

where the swelling human population exhausts the carrying capacity of the land. There is nothing uplifting about work if you
are struggling to survive. Only when there is a margin of security
and ease can you labor without fear. Only then can you freely express through work your gratitude and joy.

Sweat alone does not make work a misery. I've sweated plenty
while building houses or romping with children or digging gardens or gathering hay, and savored my labors nonetheless. Digging comes to mind because I've done a lot of that out at the cabin
these past few months. I helped Steve dig a trench where he and
Deryl could pour the footers for a porch, because Ruth and I decided we like the prospect of sitting out front and watching the
meadow bloom. I excavated for a septic tank. I dug a pit under the
edge of the cabin so that a new water pipe could be brought in below the frost line. In the fall I planted pines along the gravel
drive, and then in early January I sweated again on a subzero day
while hacking a hole in the ground to plant our Christmas tree.

Mostly when I steal away to the cabin, however, it's to go inside
and do various low jobs on the fringes of the high art practiced
by Deryl and Steve. I tear off crooked boards, pull wires through
walls, stuff insulation, install lights. Now and again I get to
swing a hammer or run the snarling miter saw. When nothing
else needs doing, I sweep the floor—the job I started with forty-
some years ago in my father's shop. And when all the sawdust
and scraps have been picked up, I lean on my broom and watch
Deryl and Steve. They stare long at a problem, consult with one
another, draw sketches, measure twice and three times, and when
they finally commit themselves to changing a roofline or hanging

a door, the results delight the mind and eye. They build as if this cabin were no mere refuge for the Sanders clan, but as if they themselves expected to live in the midst of their handiwork for the rest of their days.

Today Deryl and Steve began work on a stairway leading up to the partial second floor. When finished, the risers and treads, skirt boards and trim, will form an elaborate puzzle made of dozens of pieces of oak. Every piece must fit exactly if the stairs are to join without gaps or blemishes or squeaks. Before they make the first cut, Deryl and Steve build the whole stairway in their minds. In years to come I'll think of them whenever I climb those stairs, whenever my family and friends and I use the cabin, just as I think of them now as I hammer these letters onto the page. Their careful, skillful, scrupulous work is a standard for me to measure by, as I try to make lines with words that are as plumb and true as the lines they make with wood.

Father Within

Fifteen years after your death, you still reach through my hands whenever I saw a board or stroke a horse or plant a tree. Your country sayings rise to my lips: bright-eyed and bushy-tailed, busy as a one-armed carpenter, meaner than a junkyard dog. When I drive the back roads, my gaze goes where yours used to go, over the fields to see what's growing, into the woods to inspect the trees. Like you, I admire well-kept farms, tight fences, black soil plowed on the contour, horses in long grass, equipment in sheds out of the rain, and the sheds cleanly painted. I don't actually taste the dirt when I come to a new place, the way you did, because my tongue wouldn't know how to read the flavors, but I often take a pinch of dirt in my palm and stir it around and lift it to my face for a sniff.

I'm as old as you were, Dad, the year I graduated from college, old enough to see my body following after yours. Thinning hair, thickening waist, scarred hands. My back gives out now and again, the way yours did, from too much lifting. My shoulders ache. Your tricky knee was the left one, as I recall; mine is the right. The nose I see in the mirror when I shave may not be as flat as yours, broken seven times in boxing, but mine, broken only twice, is just as crooked. I remember noticing how veins showed like a map of rivers through the pale skin below your ankles, a surprisingly tender spot for a man so tough, and now I see the same pattern in my own feet. The same calluses, too, from our habit of going barefoot in summer.

You valued toughness. So when the pony bucked me off, I climbed back on. When the bully knocked me down, I staggered to my feet. I learned to shrug off cuts and scrapes. "Nothing that won't heal," you'd say. After a heart attack nearly finished you when I was seventeen, you never mentioned it, not once. You never complained of injuries or fatigue, never talked about your feelings at all. There I haven't been able to follow you, for when I cross a limit of worry or pain, words begin to leak from me, onto paper, into the air.

Because you scared me when you got mad, my temper isn't as hot as yours, but many of the same things get my goat. Laziness irks me, and so does sloppy workmanship. It riles me when somebody else isn't pulling his load. I hate cheats and liars, shoddy materials, and frills. I hate being late. Like you, I figure everybody ought to be ready to go when I'm ready to go, so I'll stand at the door, tapping my foot, saying, as you did, "If you're waiting on me, you're backing up."

I'm still confused about God, as you seemed to be, but I know for sure I mistrust those who claim to speak in God's name, especially on television, especially when they rant and rave and beg for big donations. "He's phony as a four-dollar bill," you'd say, waving a screwdriver at the screen. "He's crooked as a dog's hind leg." I don't like people selling me things, over the TV or on the phone or in stores. I don't like shopping, either, except for books, which you never much cared about, and lumber and hardware and tools, which you cared about a great deal. I twitch under the weight of owning things, which reminds me of how you seemed to carry house and cars and appliances and furniture on your back. When I get irritated by the latest corruption or cruelty in the day's news, I remember you grumbling as you read the paper, the way you folded each page in half with a knife-sharp crease.

You never swore in the house, and rarely swore when you knew I was within earshot. When I came dashing into the shop or barn, though, sometimes I'd hear you cursing a broken tool or stubborn pony. Then you'd cock an eyebrow at me and say, "Don't you go telling your mother. I was only exercising my vocabulary." I heard plenty of swearing at school, in locker rooms, on campouts, but none of it matched yours for music. Mine doesn't match yours, either, which is why I swear only as a last resort, when I've run through the rest of the dictionary.

I got in trouble for reading the dictionary, remember, when I drove a forklift at the factory in Louisiana and things were slow on the graveyard shift and Webster's was the only book available. The foreman said it looked mighty suspicious, a man on a forklift at midnight studying words. I know it puzzled you that I was always reading. "You're going to wear out your eyes," you'd warn me. "Watch you don't fill up your head with words and squeeze out the sense." All I ever saw you read were newspapers and how-to books, and even then you never stuck at it for long. You'd rather be running a lathe or a bird dog than sitting in a chair and running your eyes over print. My own books began to appear only after you died, so you never knew what I was up to all those years with my scribbling. Since I took up this trade, I've always wanted my writing to satisfy you, as someone who liked things honest, solid, and plain.

To remind me of how you insisted on making everything plumb and true, I keep a wooden carpenter's level on a shelf over the desk where I write. Because the shelf sags a bit under the weight of books, I slide the level back and forth until I find a spot where the bubble rests between the marks. On the same shelf there's one of the miniature wheels you made for a wagon. I often gaze at it when I'm supposed to be writing and my thoughts are wandering seven directions from Sunday; it steadies me to see those twelve spokes converging on the wooden hub. Beside the level and wheel I also keep one of the walnut jewelry boxes you made, the top inlaid with contrasting grain, and inside the box I keep the buckeyes that were in your pocket when you died. The buckeyes are dry now, hard as the nubbins of bone that showed up in your ashes. I finger the shriveled seeds every once in a while, like beads, hoping they'll keep my hands free of arthritis as you promised they would.

I'm still filling my head with words, as you can see, yet there's plenty of room for memory, if not for sense. Even though I've given up fishing since you died, I watch for likely holes in rivers and creeks. When I see branches drooping over a bank where the water runs swift and cold, I think: Dad would love to wet a hook there. Though you taught me to aim a BB gun when I was five, gave me a rifle at eight, and took me hunting with you at eleven, I never would shoot at pheasant or rabbit, squirrel or deer. That also puzzled you, I know, why I never became a hunter or a fisherman, just as it bewildered you how a boy reared with a gun in his hand could refuse to fight in Vietnam. "A pacifist?" you growled when I told you of my decision. "Where'd you learn to be a pacifist?"

I learned it from you, indirectly, because you taught me to search my conscience before I acted, and to stick by what I found there, no matter what other folks urged me to do. Like most of the standards I inherited from you, that one is too hard for me some of the time. Yet even when I ignore my conscience, I usually know what it's saying, and what you would say: "Why do you think the Lord gave us a backbone? To hold up a hat?"

There are deep ties between us, you see, however different we might appear on the surface. Although I carry binoculars in the woods instead of a shotgun, I love to stalk animals as much as you ever did. My business may be making stories rather than tires or bombs, yet I earn my living mainly by talking, just as you did in your later years. Whenever I get the chance I use my hands. I'm not half as skillful as you were, but I, too, build sheds and shelves, fix broken machines, putter around the house and yard. Because I'm warier of strangers than you were, I don't usually pick up hitchhikers on the road or help stranded motorists, but I wince with guilt as I pass them by, and like you I help my neighbors and friends as often as time and strength will allow.

I'm about 90 percent vegetarian, which would have baffled you, yet I eat with relish many of your favorite foods—watermelon, cornbread, fresh green beans, black-eyed peas, hominy grits, cheddar cheese, any kind of pie. On the other hand, your fierce appetite turned me away from smoking and drinking, the two poisons that I figured would kill you, and that finally did. Again and again in photos, a cigarette dangles from your hand. When I turned sixteen you told me I could smoke if I wanted to, but only if I was a fool. You'd started puffing at twelve, to ape the older boys, and by the time you knew better the hook was in you so deep you'd never be able to pull it out. The hook of alcohol was also deep in you, but that you wouldn't confess, not even when I caught you tipping the bottle to your lips in garage or basement or barn. "What whiskey?" you'd say in blank astonishment. "What wine?"

If I could erase one memory, it would be of the last time I confronted you about your drinking. The scene is all too clear: the two of us arguing in your shop, a few days after Christmas, a few weeks before you died. You were pretending to sand a piece of wood, leaning against the workbench because you didn't trust your legs. Your hands shook. You kept your bloodshot eyes turned away. Why couldn't you quit? I demanded. "Quit what?" you said. We can get help, I told you. "Don't need help," you muttered. I said you were selfish. I said the liquor wasn't killing only you, it was poisoning the whole family. I said you were breaking our hearts. "What're you talking about?" you mumbled. "Dad, stop lying!" I shouted, and in my anger I slammed my fist on the workbench. You lurched backwards, lifting both arms to protect your face, and I realized with dismay that you were afraid of me. Still powerful at sixty-four, barrel-chested, with a boxer's hands, you feared your son. Already hurting, you thought I was going to pile on more pain.

I never knew you to lie about anything else. Having come to the age of hard questions, I wonder now more than ever what drove you to drink. I can't bring myself to believe it was only a chemical fix. Addiction is powerful, I realize, but so were you, strong-willed and stubborn. Even as a boy I sensed there was a hunger in you, an emptiness that you tried to fill with liquor, with cigarette smoke, with gambling at cards, with boxing and fast cars, with tinkering in the shop. Now I'm sure there was a hunger in you, because I carry my own dark craving. You were silent about your fears and confusions, so I speak about mine. I fling sentences at the ache, stretch a web of words over the emptiness. What gnawed at you? What woke you before dawn and sent you prowling through the house? What made you doubt yourself, a man with more talents than time?

I suspect your doubts had something to do with being near the last of eleven children, with coming from the country and marrying a Chicago girl, and with moving north from Mississippi at a time when all white southerners were presumed to be racists. You had the best practical intelligence of anyone I've ever known, you were a state champion in mathematics, you could decipher repair manuals written half in gibberish, and yet you apologized for not graduating from college. "Would you believe, there's people working alongside me with graduate degrees!" you said uneasily. I earned the degrees for you, working my tail off, riding scholarships through famous universities where you could never have afforded to send me; yet all these years later I keep studying, keep writing, more than ever convinced of my ignorance.

In all of these ways, and more, I carry you inside me. I've also met you outside, moving around in this fleshy world. For several years after your death, whenever I saw a hefty man with blunt fingers and rust-colored hair, my heart would leap. Mind knew better, of course, but heart wasn't listening. I've tried to cure myself of seeing you on the street because, after the leap of illusion, it hurts to fall back on truth. The truth is, you're never going to lay your arm across my shoulders again. You've been exiled from the land of touch.

Strangely, I don't feel the pain of loss when I meet you in the eyes of a buck staring at me across a meadow, in the cry of a red-tailed hawk circling overhead, in the twisted limbs of a white oak, in the stamp of a horse's hoof. It's as if, having worn out your old body, you can only stick around by changing forms the way shamans do. So steady in life, in death you've become a trickster, like Raven or Coyote or Hare, flowing on in shape after shape.

I never know where you'll turn up next. Jesse and I were back-packing in the Smoky Mountains this past August, not far from your Mississippi stomping grounds. He was barely three when you died, your fourth grandchild, so he remembers you only through family stories. As we made camp in a grove of hickories and oaks that you would have admired, I was telling him about my own hikes with you. Then along toward supper time the sky turned dark and ornery with a coming storm. Before the rain hit, we decided to rig our ponchos into an awning to cover the stove. In order to stretch a line from one tree to the next, we needed to tie a pair of ropes together. I knew the best knot for the job was a sheet bend, favorite of sailors and farmers, as you explained on the day you taught it to me. I hadn't tied one in years, and so long as I stared at the ropes I couldn't remember how. Then I shut my eyes and my hands began to move, weaving the ropes; when I looked again, there was the proper knot. Jesse and I stayed dry under the awning. After we ate, he asked me to show him how to tie a sheet bend. So I did, and there you were again, reaching through my hands, reaching through his.

The Power of Stories

An American couple in their early twenties, poor graduate students traveling on a shoestring, were staying in a shabby hotel in Madrid. They knew no one in the city and knew just enough Spanish to order meals and ask directions. They often asked directions, but they had so little money that they rarely ordered meals, living instead on cheese and bread and peppers and cherries. Married only two years, instead of going out at night to shows or clubs, they lay in bed talking about what they had seen that day and reading *Don Quixote*.

On their first night in that cheap hotel, as they lay reading with heads propped against a plywood wall, they heard from the next room the sounds of a door opening and feet shuffling over carpet. Someone just beyond the flimsy wall began clearing his throat and muttering Spanish in a quavery voice that led them to guess their neighbor must be an elderly man. Soon they heard the clank and hiss of dinner preparations, as of soup boiling on a hot plate, then the clink of a spoon against a bowl, then strenuous slurping. When their neighbor began brushing his teeth and gargling, the husband and wife closed *Don Quixote,* closed their eyes, and set off in search of sleep.

Sleep was hard to find, because within minutes their neighbor began snoring. The sound reminded the wife of pumping water at her grandmother's well, and it reminded the husband of shoveling gravel into the back of a pickup truck. Eventually, after much tossing on damp sheets, they drifted off.

Along in the small hours, however, they woke suddenly to shouts from their neighbor. With their sketchy Spanish, they could make out the words "Police!" and "Help!" and "Murder!" yelled over and over again. The neighbor started pounding on the wall at the head of their bed, and the husband's heart pounded in his chest. He sat up. What to do? he wondered. Find his way over there in pajamas and run into who knows what kind of mess? Or lie there while an old man was being beaten or strangled?

Torn and trembling, as though an attacker had *him* by the throat, the husband lurched out of bed and stood on the creaky floorboards.

"We should do something," his wife said.

"I know, I know."

The husband wanted to go help, but he was afraid of leaving his wife alone, afraid of entering the dim corridor in that sleazy hotel in a strange city where he could not speak the language, afraid of the darkness. His own panting was almost as loud in his ears as the old man's shouting.

Unable to move, the husband suddenly thought: Maybe he's having a nightmare. Quickly he said his thought aloud.

"You think so?" the wife replied.

"It has to be a nightmare."

"But if it isn't?"

"It is. It must be."

While they hesitated, the yelling died down, the thrashing stopped, and presently the old man's snores resumed. The whole disturbance lasted no more than a minute, but an hour later the husband's racing heart still kept him awake.

Next morning, over a breakfast of strawberries and rolls, the wife said, "What if he'd really been in trouble?"

"He wasn't in trouble," the husband insisted.

The following night the yelling woke them again, but the husband did not get out of bed. By the third night, he only rolled over grumpily when he heard the shouts, and by the fourth night, their last in Spain, he squeezed the pillow to his ears and promptly went back to sleep.

Months and years later, the husband would remember that scene in the Madrid hotel, remember the plywood wall throbbing against his head, remember his fear; above all he would remember hesitating while a stranger in the next room begged for help. The memory stayed with him as a story, with setting and characters and voices and tumultuous feelings, all bound into a narrative. The story would often come to him when he looked at his wife or daughter or son, when he spoke with his father or mother on the phone, when he visited with a friend, when he thought of anyone whom he loved getting hurt. What he felt when the story seized him was not so much shame as a burst of clarity, about who he was and who he wished to become. Over the years, he would keep on hearing calls for help, some of which he would answer and many he would ignore; but even when he failed, the memory of that night in Madrid helped him to see his failure clearly, and from that seeing he gained courage to try again.

By now you may have guessed who the husband is. If you read obscure books, you might even have come across a version of the tale in my early collection, *Fetching the Dead*. I tell this bare-bones version now to illustrate some of the good we get from stories, and to begin saying why I consider them a source of hope.

Of all our reasons for telling and hearing stories, I want to focus here on ten: Stories entertain us. They create community. They help us to see through the eyes of other people. They show us the consequences of our actions. They educate our desires. Stories help us to dwell in place. They help us to dwell in time. They help us to deal with suffering, loss, and death. They teach us how to be human. And stories acknowledge the wonder and mystery of Creation.

Few if any stories do all of these things, nor do their effects divide neatly into the categories that I have set out. I am a categorizing animal, however, and I belong to a list-making species. The earliest surviving examples of written language are inventories of goods kept in the storehouses of ancient Mesopotamia. So let me stick with my inventory of goods, and say a few words in turn about each of these ten powers of stories.

First of all, stories entertain us. Why else do we trade them so avidly, in myths and folktales, in poems and songs, movies and plays, novels and yarns, and countless other forms? Children tell stories spontaneously, exuberantly, even before they have enough words to fill out their sentences. Anyone who has made up a story for a child, or read one from a book, only to have the child beg for it again and again, night after night, knows that the need for story goes deep in us. Scheherazade kept a sultan from putting her to death by telling him stories, always breaking off in the middle of a plot at bedtime, leaving him eager for the next installment. You do not have to be a child or a bored sultan to hunger for stories, of course, nor a captive to be saved by them. We all hunger for narrative, from the simplest anecdote or joke to the most convoluted saga, as we hunger for bread or companionship or sunlight; and we all may be fed, and even restored, by a tale that speaks to our condition.

We have been telling stories to one another for a long time, perhaps for as long as we have been using language, and we have been using language, I suspect, for as long as we have been human. More than my vested interest as a writer leads me to make that claim. Our DNA differs from that of the apes by only a few tenths of one percent, yet that small variation has led to vast differences in our way of life. Like us, apes care for their young, groom their mates, announce their territory, even wage small-scale war; but they do not write novels or compose concertos or prove theorems; they do not debate bills in legislatures or balance their accounts or fill libraries and computers with the records of their doings. "What tiny change could have had such enormous consequences?" the physiologist Jared Diamond asks in *The Third Chimpanzee;* then he goes on to say: "I can think of only one plausible answer: the anatomical basis for spoken complex language."

In all its guises, from words spoken and written to pictures and musical notes and mathematical symbols, language is our distinguishing gift, our hallmark as a species. We delight in stories because they are a playground for language, an arena for exercising this extraordinary power. The spells and enchantments that figure in so many tales remind us of the ambiguous potency in words, for creating or destroying, for binding or setting free. Italo Calvino, a wizard of storytelling, described literature as "a struggle to escape from the confines of language; it stretches out from the utmost limits of what can be said; what stirs literature is the call and attraction of what is not in the dictionary." Calvino's remark holds true, I believe, not just for the highfalutin modes we label as literature, but for every effort to make sense of our lives through narrative.

We savor that effort; we admire the display of insight and skill. We enjoy the shapeliness of stories, their lines and patterns and integrity, just as we enjoy the shapeliness of a house, a vase, a melody, a body. We are entertained by the stuff of stories as well, the romance and adventure, suspense and surprise, the solving of puzzles, the tingle of danger and salvation. The sources of our pleasure in stories are as numerous as our needs, too numerous for me to discuss them all. But a few of them will emerge as I continue through my tenfold list.

Second, stories create community. They link teller to listeners, and listeners to one another. This is obviously so when speaker and audience share the same space, as humans have done for all but the last few centuries of our million-year history, gathered around fires or huddled in huts; it is equally if less obviously so in our literate age, when we encounter more of our stories in solitude, on page or screen. When two people discover they have both read *Don Quixote,* they immediately share a piece of history, even if they happen not to have read the novel in a shabby Madrid hotel. Strangers who discover their mutual devotion to fairy tales or gangster movies or soap operas or Shakespeare's plays become thereby less strange to one another.

Frank O'Connor went so far as to declare that "the one subject a storyteller must write about" is "human loneliness." Whether or not stories speak about it directly, they offer us relief from loneliness, by revealing that our most secret feelings and thoughts do not belong to us alone, by inviting us to join the circle of readers or listeners. The strongest bonds are formed by sacred stories, which unite entire peoples. Thus Jews rehearse the events of Passover; Christians tell of a miraculous birth and death and resurrection; Buddhists tell of Gautama meditating beneath a tree; the Hopi recount the story of their emergence from the earth; the Aborigines repeat in song the primal deeds of their ancestors.

As we know only too well, sacred stories may also divide the world between those who are inside the circle and those outside, between us and them, a division that has inspired pogroms and inquisitions and wars. There is danger in story, as in any great force. If the tales that captivate us are silly or deceitful, like most of those offered by television and advertising, they waste our time and warp our desires. If they are cruel, they make us callous. If they are false and bullying, instead of drawing us into a thoughtful community they may lure us into an unthinking herd or, worst of all, into a crowd screaming for blood—in which case we need other, truer stories to renew our vision. So *The Diary of Anne Frank* and Primo Levi's *Survival in Auschwitz* are antidotes to *Mein Kampf*. So Ralph Ellison's *Invisible Man* and Toni Morrison's *Beloved* are antidotes to the paranoid yarns of the Ku Klux Klan. So the patient exchange of stories between people searching for common ground is an antidote to the hasty sloganeering and slandering of talk shows. Just as stories may rescue us from loneliness, so, by speaking to us in private, they may rescue us from mobs.

This brings me to the third item on my list, which is that stories help us to see through the eyes of other people. Here my list overlaps with one compiled by Carol Bly, who argues that the foremost gift from stories is "experience of *other*." For the duration of a story, children may sense how it feels to be old, and the elderly may recall how it feels to be young; men may try on the experiences of women, and women those of men. Through stories, we reach across the rifts not only of gender and age but of race and creed, geography and class, even the rifts between species or between enemies.

In *The Things They Carried,* Tim O'Brien takes us inside American soldiers who fought in Vietnam, yet he also gives flesh and feeling to the Vietcong, including a man whom he may or may not have killed. Whether he killed the man is not the issue, O'Brien insists; he can only contend with his guilt and grief, can only quit fighting the war, by putting a face on the enemy:

> He was a slim, dead, almost dainty young man of about twenty. He lay in the center of a red clay trail near the village of My Khe. His jaw was in his throat. His one eye was shut, the other eye was a star-shaped hole.

"What stories can do," O'Brien concludes, "is make things present."

Anyone who has read Orwell's essay "A Hanging" will recall the moment when the condemned prisoner, on his way to the gallows, walks around a mud puddle so as to keep his bare feet dry. By carefully noting that gesture, Orwell makes the stranger less alien, less menacing, more like one's own father or brother or son. By making humanly present what we fear or hate, stories resist our habit of dividing the world into us and them, friend and foe, and that is certainly cause for hope.

Folktales and fables and myths often show humans talking and working with other animals, with trees, with rivers and stones, as if recalling or envisioning a time of easy commerce among all beings. Helpful ducks and cats and frogs, wise dragons, stolid oaks, venturesome winds, faithful rocks, all have lessons for us in these old tales. The trickster—Coyote or Raven or Hare— changes form as rapidly as clouds, reminding us how fluid nature is, and how arbitrary are the divisions between human and beast, between self and other. It is as if through language, the very power that estranges us from other creatures, we are slowly working our way back into communion with the rest of nature.

Of course no storyteller can literally become hawk or pine, any more than a man can become a woman, or a white person change skins with a black; we cross those boundaries only imperfectly, through leaps of imagination. "Could a greater miracle take place than for us to look through each other's eyes for an instant?" Thoreau asks. We come nearer to achieving that miracle in stories than anywhere else. "It is not natural for our minds to be open to what is *other,*" Carol Bly points out, "we have to cultivate it." Stories cultivate that openness. They release us from the confines of self. They nurture compassion and empathy, which are the springs of justice and kindness.

A fourth power of stories is to show us the consequences of our actions. Plots are more formal versions of the scenarios that we project all the time: if I cook a whole chicken for dinner tonight, I can use the leftovers for soup tomorrow. If I poison the dandelions, I may kill the goldfinches. If I ride my bicycle instead of driving, I can park right next to the library; but if it rains later on I'll get soaked, and in any case I won't be able to offer Mrs. Thomas a lift home.

We are constantly thinking through sequences of actions, from simple ones such as how to hold two armloads of groceries while opening a door, to complex ones such as how to build a barn or rear a child or govern a country. As in our everyday scenarios, stories try out choices in the lives of characters, then trace the results. A durable story is one that persuades audiences, generation after generation, of the truth of its findings.

To act responsibly, we must be able to foresee where our actions might lead; and stories train our sight. They reveal the patterns of human conduct, from motive through action to result. Whether or not a story has a moral purpose, therefore, it cannot help but have a moral effect, for better or worse. This link between fiction and morality has been denied by some writers—notably by those who, like Joyce, feared the tyranny of church or state; but it has been upheld by many others, from Tolstoy and Dickens and Chekhov to Faulkner and Baldwin and Gordimer. The old debate was repeated in the June 1988 pages of *Harper's,* where William Gass maintained that art is amoral, Robert Stone responding that

> Any fictional work of serious intent argues for the significance of its story. A reader holds the characters in judgment, investing sympathy or withholding it, always alert for recognitions, hoping to see his lonely state reflected across time, space, and circumstance. How then can fiction ever be independent of morality?

An Apache elder, quoted by the anthropologist Keith Basso, puts the case more directly: "Stories go to work on you like arrows. Stories make you live right. Stories make you replace yourself." Stories do work on us, on our minds and hearts, showing us how we might act, who we might become, and why.

So we arrive at a fifth power of stories, which is to educate our desires. The root meaning of *educate* is to lead out, as if everything a student learns were already inside, waiting to be released. While I doubt that we are born carrying the formulas of calculus or the spellings of English words, I believe that we do carry from birth certain hungers and fears. Advertisers and dictators and hate mongers tap these innate emotions to sell their products or their party lines. Look how easily our desire for beauty and sophistication may be invested in cigarettes, how our desire for grace and speed may be invested in cars, how our desire for safety and power may be invested in guns. There is nothing wrong with those desires, yet the goals toward which they are often aimed, by merchants or zealots, may be disastrous.

Instead of playing on our selfishness and fear, stories can give us images of what is truly worth seeking, worth having, worth doing. I mean here something more than the way fairy tales repeat our familiar longings. I mean the way *Huckleberry Finn* makes us want to be faithful, the way *Walden* makes us yearn to confront the essential facts of life, the way *Mrs. Dalloway* teaches us to treasure words, the way *Pilgrim at Tinker Creek* wakes us to our surroundings; I mean the way *Cry, the Beloved Country* makes us long to forgive those who have hurt us and to ask forgiveness from those whom we have hurt; I mean the way tales by Ivan Turgenev or Grace Paley or Doris Lessing or Gabriel García Márquez persuade us to pay loving attention to neighbors and strangers. What stories at their best can do is lead our desires in new directions—away from greed, toward generosity; away from suspicion, toward sympathy; away from an obsession with material goods, so dear to a consumer culture, and toward a concern for spiritual goods.

———

One of the spiritual goods I cherish is the peace of being at home, in family and neighborhood and community and landscape. Much of what I know about becoming intimate with one's home ground I have learned from reading the tales of indigenous peoples and the testaments of individuals who have decided to stay put. The list of my teachers is long; a short list would include Lao-tzu and Thoreau and Faulkner, Thomas Merton, Black Elk, Aldo Leopold, Rachel Carson, Gary Snyder, and Wendell Berry. Their work exemplifies the sixth power of stories, which is to help us dwell in place.

According to Eudora Welty, herself a deeply rooted storyteller, "the art that speaks most clearly, explicitly, directly and passionately from its place of origin will remain the longest understood." So we return to the epic of Gilgamesh, with its brooding on the forests and rivers of Babylonia; we return to the ancient Hebrew accounts of a land flowing with milk and honey; we follow the Aboriginal songs of journeys over the continent of Australia, and Inuit tales of survival in the Arctic, as we return to Hardy's novels about Wessex and Frost's poems about the Green Mountains—because they all convey a passionate knowledge of place.

Such knowledge may be the salvation of a place, as of those who dwell there. Near the end of his first term, President Clinton signed an order designating some two million acres of the red rock country of Utah as a national monument. That land has long been treasured in stories, from the pictographs of the Anasazi to a book of testimonials by nature writers submitted to Congress a few months ago. In making the announcement, the president gave his own testimony:

And one of the happiest memories of my entire life was when, for some flukey reason, even in the summertime, I found a place on a rock overlooking the Grand Canyon where I was all alone. And for two hours I sat and I lay down on that rock and I watched the sunset. And I watched the colors change layer after layer after layer for two hours. I could have sat there for two days if the sun had just taken a little longer to set. And even today, 25 years later, in hectic, crazy times, in lonely, painful times, my mind drifts back to those two hours that I was alone on that rock watching the sunset over this canyon. And it will be with me till the day I die.

There is more than politics in that recollection. Only someone who has never been moved by an encounter with the land could fail to hear the ring of genuine attachment in the president's story.

We need to nourish that emotion, in person after person, if we hope to redeem the land from the weight of our numbers and the pressure of our hungers. "To preserve our places and to be at home in them, it is necessary to fill them with imagination," says Wendell Berry in *Standing by Words,* "to see them first clearly with the eyes, and then to see them with the imagination in their sanctity, as belonging to the Creation."

The Lakota, Navajo, Iroquois and other Native American tribes ground their stories in nearby fields and rivers and mountains, and thus carry their places in mind. As the Pueblo travel in their homeland, according to Leslie Marmon Silko, they recall the stories that belong to each mesa and arroyo, and "Thus the continuity and accuracy of the oral narratives are reinforced by the landscape—and the Pueblo interpretation of that landscape is *maintained.*"

Before the coming of Europeans, most of our continent was

covered with names that were shorthand versions of stories—about the gifts of a place, about memorable events that happened there, about other creatures that lived there. Here are some examples, gathered and translated by Richard Nelson from the Inupiaq and Koyukon of Alaska: Where a Caribou Is Lying on Its Belly, Where the Blackfish Run in Season, Where a Forest Fire Burned the Hill to the River, Where the Great Raven Traversed the Length of a Lake, Where a Standing Thing Fell and Left Its Traces, Place to Hunt Polar Bears, High Place Where You Look Out at the Land.

We all need vantage points for looking out at the land, and stories of place may provide them. They help us recognize that we belong to the earth, blood and brain and bone, and that we are kin to other creatures. Life has never been easy, yet in every continent we find tales of a primordial garden, an era of harmony and bounty, a golden age. In *A God Within,* René Dubos suggests that these old tales might be recollections "of a very distant past when certain groups of people had achieved biological fitness to their environment." Whether or not our ancestors ever lived in ecological balance, if we aspire to do so in the future, we must nourish the affectionate, imaginative bond between person and place.

Mention of past and future brings us to the seventh power of stories, which is to help us dwell in time. I am thinking here not so much of the mechanical time parceled out by clocks, as of historical and psychological time. History is public, a tale of influences and events that have shaped the present; the mind's time is private, a flow of memory and anticipation that continues, in eddies and rapids, for as long as we are conscious. Narrative orients us in both kinds of time, private and public, by linking before and after within the lives of characters and communities, by showing action leading on to action, moment to moment, beginning to middle to end.

Once again we come upon the tacit morality of stories, for moral judgment relies, as narrative does, on a belief in cause and effect. Stories teach us that every gesture, every act, every choice we make sends ripples of influence into the future. Thus we hear that the caribou will only keep giving themselves to the hunter if the hunter kills them humbly and respectfully. We hear that salmon will spawn only so long as people honor the river. We hear that love usually breeds love, and hate always breeds hate. We hear that the enemy one shoots in battle will die again and again in one's heart. We hear that all our deeds are recorded in some heavenly book, in the grain of the universe, in the mind of God, and that everything we sow we shall reap.

Stories gather experience into shapes we can hold and pass on through time, much the way DNA molecules in our cells record genetic discoveries and pass them on from generation to generation. Until the invention of writing, the discoveries of the tribe were preserved and transmitted by storytellers, above all by elders. "Under hunter-gatherer conditions," Jared Diamond observes, "the knowledge possessed by even one person over the age of seventy could spell the difference between survival and starvation for a whole clan."

Anyone who visits a mall or walks the mean streets of our cities might suspect that we are still hunter-gatherers; at any rate, we still need the lore that stories preserve. Ursula Le Guin suggests that we think of stories as carrier bags: like bellies or baskets, like houses or wombs, like the great sack of the cosmos itself, they are containers for holding something vital. If you know someone who has lost touch with past and future, because of disease or injury or age, you will realize that, of all the gifts contained in stories, nothing is more vital than the ability to navigate in time.

Aware of time passing, however, we mourn things passing away, and we often fear the shape of things to come. Hence our need for the eighth power of stories, which is to help us deal with suffering, loss, and death.

From the Psalms to the Sunday comics, many tales comfort the fearful and the grieving; they show the downtrodden rising up, the weak triumphing over the strong, love winning out over hatred, laughter defying misery. It is easy to dismiss this hopefulness as escapism, but as Italo Calvino reminds us, "For a prisoner, to escape has always been a good thing, and an individual escape can be a first necessary step toward a collective escape."

Aristotle, with his theory of catharsis, is only one in a long line of commentators who have recognized the healing power of stories. I have in mind here the root meaning of healing, which is to make whole. In *The Call of Stories,* Robert Coles argues that it is less important to fit psychiatric patients into abstract medical categories than to understand "the concrete details of a given person's narrative." His own practice, as writer and physician, like that of Freud and Jung, is founded on the exchange of stories. "The whole point of stories," says Coles, "is not 'solutions' or 'resolutions' but a broadening and even a heightening of our struggles—with new protagonists and antagonists introduced, with new sources of concern or apprehension or hope."

Those who have walked through the valley of the shadow of

death, who have witnessed horrors, tell stories as a way of fending off despair: thus Primo Levi tells of surviving Auschwitz and Aleksandr Solzhenitsyn tells of surviving the Soviet Gulag by recalling the fates of their fellow prisoners; James Baldwin and Toni Morrison recount the anguish of plantation and ghetto; Black Elk tells about the slaughter of the buffalo, the loss of his Lakota homeland, and the scattering of his people; Joseph Heller and Tim O'Brien narrate the atrocities of war; Martin Buber retells the stories of Hasidic Jews as a way of preserving faith amidst desolation. As Baldwin says, "While the tale of how we suffer, and how we are delighted, and how we may triumph is never new, it always must be heard. There isn't any other tale to tell, it's the only light we've got in all this darkness."

Those of us who have not lived through horrors must still face losing all that we love, including our own lives. Stories reek of our obsession with mortality, not only in thrillers and mysteries, but in the countless movies and plays and tales of all kinds that end, as our lives do, in death. As the most enchanting first line of a tale is "Once upon a time," so the most comforting last line is "and they lived happily ever after." This fairy-tale formula expresses a deep longing not only for happiness, but for ever-afterness, for an assurance that life as well as happiness will endure, that it will survive all challenges, perhaps even the grave. We feel the force of that longing, whether or not we believe that it can ever be fulfilled.

The ninth item on my list is really a summation of all that I have said thus far: stories teach us how to be human. As I understand it, becoming fully human means learning to savor the world, to share in community, to see through the eyes of other people, to take responsibility for our actions, to educate our desires, to dwell knowingly in time and place, to cope with suffering and death. We are creatures of instinct, but not solely of instinct. More than any other animal we must *learn* how to behave. In this perennial effort, as Le Guin says, "Story is our nearest and dearest way of understanding our lives and finding our way onward." Skill is knowing how to do something; wisdom is knowing when and why to do it, or to refrain from doing it. While stories may display skill aplenty, in technique or character or plot, what the best of them offer is wisdom. They hold a living reservoir of human possibilities, telling us what has worked before, what has failed, where meaning and purpose and joy might be found. At the heart of many tales is a test, a puzzle, a riddle, a problem to solve; and that, surely, is the condition of our lives, both in detail—as we decide how to act in the present moment—and in general, as we seek to understand what it all means. Like so many characters, we are lost in a dark wood, a labyrinth, a swamp, and we need a trail of stories to show us the way back to our true home.

Our ultimate home is the Creation, and anyone who pretends to comprehend this vast and intricate abode is either a lunatic or a liar. In spite of all that we have learned through millennia of inquiry, we still dwell in mystery. Why there is a universe, why we are here, why there is life or consciousness at all, where if anywhere the whole show is headed—these are questions for which we have no final answers. Not even the wisest of tales can tell us.

The wisest, in fact, acknowledge the wonder and mystery of Creation—and that is the tenth power of stories.

In the beginning, we say, *at the end of time,* we say, but we are only guessing. "I think one should work into a story the idea of not being sure of all things," Borges advised, "because that's the way reality is." The magic and romance, the devils and divinities we imagine, are pale tokens of the forces at play around us. The elegant, infinite details of the world's unfolding, the sheer existence of hand or tree or star, are more marvelous than anything we can say about them.

The Romantics were fond of comparing our acts of imagination with God's act of creating the universe, but that is to flatter ourselves. Still, the analogy between small and great minds is alluring. A number of modern physicists have suggested that the more we learn about the universe, the more it seems like an immense, sustained, infinitely subtle flow of consciousness—the more it seems, in fact, like a grand story, lavishly imagined and set moving. Scriptures speak of God's thoughts as if we could read them; but we read only by the dim light of a tricky brain on a young planet near a middling star. Nonetheless, we need these cosmic narratives, however imperfect they may be, however filled with guesswork. So long as they remain open to new vision, so long as they are filled with awe, they give us hope of finding meaning within the great mystery.

I went to sleep wondering how to speak about hope, and I woke up knowing I must begin with stories. We need one another. Yet our souls and communities are divided by fear and ignorance and strife. We walk in beauty, yet much of what we do is ugly. We inhabit a magnificent planet, yet we devour our home. Stories are not instruction manuals; they do not teach us in any simple way how to lead our lives. By inviting us to participate in imaginary lives, however, they deepen our understanding and enlarge our sympathies for other people, for other creatures, for the places and purposes that human beings share, and for the earth. That is a good beginning.

Witnessing to a Shared World

Good fiction tells us what sort of creatures we are, what life is like, or what it might be like, and how things look and taste and feel. Good nonfiction does the same. Then what makes it *non*? What do we mean by that sly negative prefix? Fiction is not flat-out lying, as Mark Twain liked to say it was. If there weren't some truth in stories and novels, some ring of authenticity, we wouldn't keep reading them. But fiction *is* a fabrication, made up out of anything and everything the writer sees or recollects or imagines. That license to make things up is implicit in the name itself, for the Latin *fictio* means a counterfeiting. Even the most faithful historical novel, which draws on events that actually happened and on people who actually lived, fills in gaps between the facts with material of the author's own invention. If a novel is entertaining or illuminating, we accept the make-believe and stay around for the show. Reading fiction, we don't assume that everything happening on the page once happened off the page; we don't assume that when the narrator says "I," it's the author speaking.

In reading a personal essay, a memoir, or the report of a journey, however, that is precisely what we do assume. When a piece of writing announces itself to be nonfiction—a claim that may appear in the text, on the dust jacket, or in a contributor's note— the author is tacitly promising not to be making things up from scratch, but to be drawing honestly on real events, and the author is also agreeing to be held accountable for everything uttered by that slender, upright "I."

Let me make it clear that I'm speaking about *personal* nonfiction, work that springs from the writer's own experience and that grants the writer a significant role in the story. I'm not concerned here with the many worthy but *im*personal forms of nonfiction, from biographies and histories to telephone directories and ingredients labels on the sides of cereal boxes. We can test the veracity of these impersonal forms—by reading other books on the same subject, for example, by dialing a listed number, or by running a sample of cereal through a chromatograph, but most of the time we take their authority for granted. Although scholarly books, news reports, how-to manuals, and encyclopedias are written by flesh-and-blood people, such works usually don't emphasize the author's own role in gathering and shaping and evaluating the material; they don't disclose what is at stake for the one who sets down the words. By contrast, personal nonfiction calls attention to the way the material has been filtered by the writer's consciousness, and it reveals how the tale affects the teller. Because the material of personal nonfiction is often private, known only to a few people, or perhaps only to the author alone, we may not be able to check it for accuracy against other sources, so we must take these private reports on trust if we are to take them at all.

What sort of trust? What are we being asked to believe? These questions bring us back to that slippery contrast with fiction. In fiction, the relation between the words on the page and the world outside the page is loose and easy; the writer is free to follow wherever imagination leads. The only curb on the writer's freedom is the necessity of persuading the reader to tag along. Indeed, the very arbitrariness of fiction, its untethered playfulness, has been one of the perennial themes of fiction-makers, from Cervantes and Sterne to Calvino and Borges and Barth.

In nonfiction, however, the relations between words and world are more constrained—or at least they're supposed to be. When scholars find out that some famous autobiographer has rewritten the past in a high-handed way, perhaps laying claim to triumphs that never happened or denying awkward events that did happen, they blow the whistle. It's harder to check the accuracy of personal nonfiction when the person is obscure, as I am, yet the contract with the reader is the same. When I speak to you on the page, you should be able to assume that I'm telling you the truth, as nearly as I can recall it, discover it, or understand it. Of course I may be lying through my teeth, or I may simply be deluded, but that only means I've broken the contract. My dishonesty or delusion no more abolishes the implicit agreement between writer and reader than a spouse's infidelity abolishes marriage.

Let me push the marriage analogy a bit farther. I remain faithful to my wife not because I'm afraid she'll find out if I have an affair but because I love her, because I'm joined to her by ties both subtle and strong. My fidelity is an orientation of the heart. Similarly, when I write about my family, my neighbors, my town, or my region; when I write about owls or otters, about serving on a jury or savoring a meal, about stroking a horse or wiring a house; when I write about meeting my father after his death in the guise of a red-tailed hawk; when I write about mourning a friend or making a home or searching for God; when I write about anything that engages me deeply, I try to be faithful to my perceptions, to what I have actually seen and heard, not because I figure some sleuth might check up on me, but because I'm devoted to my subjects. I choose to be a witness rather than an inventor. I feel accountable to a reality outside myself, to people, to places, to events large and small, to powers for which I have no name.

It has become fashionable in some literary circles to claim that there is no reality outside the self, at least none that can be reliably known. According to this view, all writing is necessarily fiction, even history, even science, not to mention the personal essay. Anyone who believes, as I do, in a world independent of one's own subjectivity is dismissed as a naive realist. I suspect, however, that those who do the dismissing, hug their own children as precious beings rather than as clever fabrications; I suspect they fill their bellies with food, just as if they needed nourishment to stay alive; I suspect they avoid jumping out of windows for fear of falling; I suspect they count on being able to withdraw money from their pension funds after they retire. In short, although it's easy to pretend that "reality" is whatever we choose to make it, we all behave, in our sane hours, as if the world stubbornly resists manipulation by our minds.

Though firmly tethered to that resilient world, nonfiction is still art. It selects, interprets, shapes. No piece of writing, no matter how faithful to its sources, can be a pure transcription of experience. Words and world are two distinct realms. Language offers only a semblance of life.

The closest I've come to setting down experience directly on the page is in an essay called "Doing Time in the Thirteenth Chair," from my book *The Paradise of Bombs*. While serving as an alternate juror, sitting by my lonesome on a chair between the jury box and the witness stand, I scribbled notes on small yellow pads about everything that happened during the five days of a drug-dealing trial. I described all the participants, the courtroom, the atmosphere; I chronicled the sequence of witnesses; I copied down whole swatches of testimony. Each night, I smuggled the yellow pads home with me and typed out fuller versions of my scribbles.

By week's end I had about fifty pages of notes, yet I knew they left out many nuances, many gestures, chunks of background and entire biographies. I also realized that every page of notes bore my slant on events, my reactions to character, my estimates of guilt or innocence. Before the lawyers finished their opening arguments, my own history had become entangled with that of the defendant. This tangle, in fact, was what set me writing. I wasn't merely reporting this trial, like a journalist assigned to the courthouse; I was *living* it. I was an interested party. In composing the essay, therefore, I had to say how I was drawn into the drama. I had to admit my ignorance and my biases, so far as I recognized them. While I wrote, notions and images that had not occurred to me during the trial made their way onto the page. I ended up using only a selection of my already partial notes, leaving out whatever seemed irrelevant to the story I was telling.

And where did the story come from? Finding a trail through the welter of events is always the result of imagination and reflection as well as perception. Merely choosing what to write about, from all the subjects under the sun, is an imperial act. I chose to write about this trial because it fascinated me. Thus, while all the characters in my essay are real people, and the defendant is really serving a long hitch in prison, and all the words I attribute to witnesses were copied down as they spoke, "Doing Time in the Thirteenth Chair" is still a highly personal account. Every sentence is a translation of life into language, and it carries the accent of the translator.

I rarely have a padful of on-the-spot notes to work from when I'm writing. More often I'm working from memory—of something that happened yesterday or last summer or thirty years ago—and memory is notoriously tricky. Ask five people who saw a bank robbery to describe the thief, and you're likely to get five descriptions, some of them contradictory. Memory edits and revises the past, erasing portions, moving things around, filling in gaps, and, yes, even manufacturing pieces. In writing from memory, therefore, the best one can do is to search diligently, to check one's own recollections against those of other people, when that's possible, and to acknowledge to the reader one's uncertainty. The reader, in turn, should recognize that nonfiction made from memory never gives us the past but only a version of the past.

A few years ago, I returned to a hamlet in Ohio where as a boy I had brushed against several great mysteries, including death and sex and God. On this return visit, I walked idly around the crossroads settlement of Wayland, from the parsonage to the cider-pressing house, from a horse pasture to my biology teacher's meadow, from a high school girlfriend's backyard to a Methodist church, and each spot brought back a surge of memories. I had no intention of writing about the visit. During the long drive back home to southern Indiana, however, the place kept floating in my mind, luminous with meaning, and the people I had known there kept speaking, and the mysteries I had first encountered there kept beckoning. So as I cruised the interstate I found myself composing, scene by scene, the essay that would become "Wayland." It is all a tissue of memory. How slippery that tissue may be, how deceptive, how distorted by time and distance, no one knows better than I. And so I confess as much in the essay itself.

For all the inevitable biases, for all the lapses and illusions, for all the artifice, "Wayland" and "Doing Time in the Thirteenth Chair," like dozens of other essays I've written, still owe allegiance to a reality that I did not make up. When I'm at work on such pieces, I never forget that a shared world precedes and surrounds and ultimately measures the worth of everything I write. I mull over these matters as someone who wrote nothing but short stories and novels for a dozen years before taking up the personal essay. Writing fiction, I am most aware of the free play of mind; writing nonfiction, I am most aware of the stubborn resistance of the world. There may be nothing on the page to distinguish an essay from a first-person short story, since nonfiction may use any device of form or style that fiction uses. Where the two modes differ is in the writer's attitude toward the sources that give rise to words. Fidelity to life outside the page does not make nonfiction more virtuous than fiction, nor more important, nor more true. It merely enforces on the writer the stringent discipline of bearing witness.

Who Speaks on the Page?

When I slouched in my ink-stained seat, in third or sixth or tenth grade, and muttered a wisecrack to the students nearby, a teacher with ears tuned to the sly voices of children would invariably demand, "Who's talking?" Whether or not I put up my hand to confess, the teacher's gaze would soon light on me, and he or she would ask the withering follow-up question: "If you have something to say, Scott, why don't you share it with the whole class?"

What I had to say was rarely worth the attention of the whole class. Spoken aloud to the hushed room, my wisecrack sounded anything but wise. Usually it sounded rude, lame, or cheap. The lesson I learned from those painful episodes was that I should be mighty careful about the words I spoke, since there was always a chance I'd wind up delivering them to an audience. Any time I opened my mouth to speak, I might be held accountable for what I said.

Meanwhile, from the same teachers, I was learning a contrary lesson about writing. We can't help giving ourselves away in speech, but in writing, I gathered, we should aim to disguise the quirky, opinionated, memory-laden self who sets words down on the page. Year after year, teachers struck pencil marks through my private fancies, my images and metaphors, my homely examples drawn from the farm life I knew on the back roads of Ohio, my heartfelt notions and wild speculations. They made it clear that I was not to compare the pleasure of figuring out a poem to the baying of coon dogs hot on the scent, nor to discuss immigration by quoting the Old World sayings of my Assyrian grandfather, nor to describe the excitement of a presidential campaign by recalling the day when the Lollums' shack burned down with Mr. Lollum inside, drunk as a skunk. Anything that made me sound different from the general run of my classmates was pruned away, first by my teachers and then by me. Over those same years, of course, my classmates were having their own wings clipped.

When I wrote in a paper on the Civil War that Sherman's bloody march to the sea reminded me of a deer hunt at the arsenal where my father worked, the tired and kindly man who rode herd over our rowdy seventh grade told me to leave out my private thoughts and stick to the facts. The facts had been recorded long ago and far away, and my job was to dig them up, copy them onto note cards, shuffle the cards into a plausible order, and then march straight through, quoting and paraphrasing, as ruthlessly as Sherman on his way through Georgia. What I felt about the burned cities or the bloodshed, what I thought about slavery, what I knew of my father's white Mississippi kinfolk or their black neighbors, had no place in a school paper about the Civil War. There was no place, either, for the lunch-counter sit-ins, bus boycotts, and pitched battles over school desegregation that I witnessed on the evening news.

About the time I graduated from scrawling with a fat pencil to scrawling with a slender one, I also graduated from using the first-person singular. I learned to compose entire essays without revealing who gathered the evidence, constructed the argument, arrived at the judgments, or chose the words. "One has reason to assume," I wrote, or "Thus we see," or "An interesting point to observe is that," or "A majority of experts agrees." I became slick at hypothetical phrasing, in which equivocal, unattributable views dangled from that handy weasel word "it": "It might be concluded," "It would seem to be the case," "It may well have been otherwise." I learned to compose sentences in which abstractions appear to maneuver on their own, without any human actors: "A tragedy occurred." "Profits rose sharply on news of the takeover." "The agreement fell apart." "War broke out." I became adept at the passive voice, that essential tool of bureaucrats, corporate pirates, and flimflam artists: "The village was destroyed." "Funding has been eliminated." "The factory will be closed, and the jobs will be moved to Mexico." Who trashed the village, cut the funding, shut the factory? Who knows?

I don't blame my teachers for training me in this mealymouthed and evasive manner of writing. They were only preparing me, as well as they knew how, for the sort of writing they imagined I would have to do for the rest of my life. Indeed, their training served me well right through graduate school to a Ph.D. and tenure in a college English department, and would have served me well enough had I gone on to a career in law, science, medicine, business, foreign service, or government. By the end of high school, for example, I could have written speeches for the tobacco barons, who gabble away without ever admitting their complicity in murder; I could have written Pentagon manuals on the launching of nuclear missiles, as calmly as if I were describing the heaving of baseballs; I could have written press releases designed to confuse the public, such as a recent one from the

White House that dealt with a scandal by conceding that "mistakes were made," without bothering to reveal who made the mistakes, or when, or why.

I learned to write clean, clear sentences when lucidity was called for, but I also learned to write sentences so murky that even a veteran grammarian could not have diagramed them. When I was uncertain of my ground, or merely bored, I could always hide in the verbal thickets and dare the reader to track me down. I learned how to camouflage my own views behind those of the authorities I quoted. During my long apprenticeship in school, I mastered the anonymous prose that mumbles like elevator music in the background of our industrial civilization—the prose of memos, quarterly reports, grant proposals, program summaries, newscasts, run-of-the-mill journalism, court briefs, perfunctory scholarship, and tidy English papers.

The only trouble was that even as a schoolboy I hated reading or writing anonymous prose. I loved language with the juice still in it and the bark still on it, language that conveyed the rhythm and reach of an individual voice. So I lugged home from the library books whose meanings were largely a mystery to me, but whose sentences rang in my head with a distinctive music. Mark Twain, Walt Whitman, Emily Dickinson, William Faulkner, D. H. Lawrence, Flannery O'Connor, James Joyce, William Butler Yeats, and William Carlos Williams may never have had a more baffled or word-drunk young reader than I was. When our class read *Macbeth* or *Moby-Dick,* I didn't want to write the zillionth numb commentary on the novel or play: I wanted to write a novel or play of my own.

Stories and poems affected me in the same subversive way. By the time I was in college, majoring in physics for a spell before switching to English, I dutifully wrote formal essays for class, but in private I wrote fiction and poetry that broke all the laws of school. In that private writing I tried on the voices from books that infatuated me, I lowered the verbal masks and spoke of what amazed and bewildered me, I brooded on my brief and mysterious life.

In graduate school, I began dividing my days between academic writing, for which I had received a scholarship, and personal writing, for which I received only the secret delight of fitting language to the world. I started getting up at five or six and working until eight or so on stories, and then I would labor from breakfast until bedtime on my dissertation. Hardly a day went by without my thinking that the subject of that dissertation, D. H. Lawrence, would have howled in scorn at the solemn books of criticism written about him, including my own.

Still, I finished my book on Lawrence, found a publisher, found a job, and, in 1971, set up as a teacher at Indiana University. I have remained at Indiana ever since, because it proved to be a hospitable place, where I've been permitted to go through the slow conversion from critic to storyteller, although not without provoking some of my colleagues to scratch their heads.

After I began teaching, the portion of my days given over to fiction kept growing, and the portion given over to criticism kept shrinking. Before the tenure clock ticked through six years, I had given up anonymous prose entirely. In stories, novels, book reviews, and personal essays, I was flouting the rules I had learned about writing in school. I played with sound, strung images together line after line, flung out metaphors by the handful. Sin of sins, I even mixed metaphors, the way any fertile field will sprout dozens of species of grass and flower and fern. I let my feelings show. I dragged in characters from the back roads of Ohio, the bayous of Louisiana, or the mountains of Oregon, from London or Paris or Madrid, and from any other place I'd visited. I summoned up memories. I drew shamelessly on my own life. I swore off jargon and muddle and murk. I wrote in the active voice, and as nearly as I could in my own voice, the one I used for speaking about matters close to my heart.

My way of teaching changed more slowly than my way of writing. For a while I felt duty bound to train my students as I had been trained, in case they might one day need to write dry dissertations or bland quarterly reports or enigmatic memos. But I soon realized how phony it was for me to encourage a kind of writing that I could not bear to read. So I began asking my students to write in the first-person singular. Instead of "One might deduce from the foregoing examples," I would suggest: How about "I think"? Instead of "The white whale inspires dread in the reader," try "The white whale scares me." I began inviting my students to draw on their own experience, whenever appropriate, as a way of tying their studies to their life. If a girl you knew in high school killed herself after a tiff with a boy, how could you keep that out of a paper on *Romeo and Juliet*? If the light went out in your father's eyes after he was laid off, surely that belonged in a paper on *Death of a Salesman*. I told my students to avoid jargon, unless no familiar word would serve, and then to explain the unfamiliar word in terms that common readers could understand. I warned them to avoid passive constructions, except in dire necessity, and to make clear, in every sentence containing an action or a judgment, just who was acting or judging.

In my early years of teaching, some students balked at this advice, and some still do. They have been told it's arrogant or callow to say "I" on the page, yet here I am asking them to vouch for every syllable they put down. They have worked hard to build up their vocabularies, yet here I am saying never use a fifty-cent word when a nickel one will do. After receiving A's for fancy phrases, they don't like receiving C's because I find the phrases empty. After learning to wrap the views of experts into neat packages from which their own views have been carefully omitted, some students are dismayed when I insist on hearing what they themselves think about the hard questions. It is as though writing has been for them a game played with hollow figures lined up on a blank field, abstract and safe, and now here I am insisting that writers must climb onto the page and risk their own necks.

Most students, however, seem to welcome the chance of writing more personally, more concretely, more passionately. So invited, they often produce essays that are lively and engaged, a pleasure to read—often, but by no means always. In spite of my best advice and the students' own best efforts, sometimes their essays remain stiff and dull. What goes wrong? Most commonly, I think, the problem is tone-deafness. Good prose is a kind of speech, more deliberate and shapely than the words we utter aloud, yet still akin to the living voice. Anyone who writes well, I suspect, writes primarily by ear, listening to the music of words. That means we should be careful what language we allow to tune our ears. If you've grown up in the midst of gifted talkers, then you're in luck; but if the talk you hear comes mainly from television or movies, if you read mostly junk, or if you don't read much at all, you're not likely to develop a keen ear for your own writing. You won't be able to hear the clunks and clichés. You won't know whether your sentences are breathing.

My struggles in helping students learn to write more vividly and honestly have deepened my sympathy for my own teachers, who were always burdened with too many classes and too many papers. There is no short cut to good writing, no list of ten easy steps. I am biased, of course, but I believe that writing is the most difficult art that most of us ever try to learn, which is why relatively few of us ever learn it very well.

The best writers I've worked with over the years have been the most adventurous and discriminating readers. I've never figured out how to turn a nonreader or a junk-reader into a good writer. But no matter how dull or sharp their ear for language, if I can persuade students to think of writing as their own voice on the page, if I can persuade them to take responsibility for everything they put down, they are far more likely to produce work that they and I will care to read. So time and again, I pencil in the margins of their papers: What do *you* think? What do you feel? How does this bear on your own experience? These questions are only variations on the one my teachers put to me when I whispered wisecracks in class: *Who's talking?*

I am aware of two major objections to this call for personal writing, the first one practical and the second philosophical. The practical objection is that we need people skilled in *im*personal writing. I agree. We need writers capable of producing rigorous science, disciplined scholarship, balanced journalism. We need writers who can translate knowledge into reports and newsletters and instruction manuals, without intruding their own opinions or quirks. A civilization based on information requires legions of people who can present that information efficiently, with a minimum display of self. But even if the self is not on display, an actual flesh-and-blood human being still composes the sentences, and writers well-trained in the first-person singular are likelier to feel a responsibility for the accuracy and impact of their words.

The philosophical objection is that the self is an illusion, and hence there is no person in personal writing. I'm not equipped to answer the philosophers, even if I had the space to do so. I can only say I flatly disagree with any theory that would turn the individual into a puppet whose strings are tugged by outside forces —by race and gender and class, by advertising and the mass media, by genetic codes and the unconscious, by language itself. Granted, the self is a sometimes fragile construction that responds to many influences, yet it remains a moral center. Individuals pull voting levers and pull triggers, go to bat and go to jail, pay taxes, apply for fellowships, publish books, fall in love, give birth to children, and mourn their dead. Unless we are willing to quit holding individuals accountable for their actions, we should hold them accountable for their words.

To Eva, on Your Marriage

Soon you'll walk down the aisle with a dancer's grace, your hand looped through my arm, and the minister will ask who gives this bride away. I will obey custom and your firm instructions by saying "I do," yet I can't give you away, for you aren't mine to give. You belong only to yourself, and to the power that created you, so beautiful and bright, out of sunlight, food, water, and air.

For me to claim ownership of you, as fathers since time out of mind have claimed ownership of their daughters, would be like a twig on a great oak pretending to have made all by itself the newest bud. You're a sprout of the whole tree; you're the daughter of Earth. Yes, I contributed my share to your making, passing on my genes through an act of delight. But this joining with your mother to set you in motion gives me no right of possession, for the biological memory carried in my genes stretches back, unbroken, through the countless inventions of eye and hand and backbone and brain to the first flicker of life in the primal seas.

I knew you, darling, while you swam and kicked in the small sea of your mother's womb. I knew you from laying my fingers and ear to her taut belly. I knew you from the shining in her eyes and from the catch in her breath when you moved. All that summer and fall of 1972, while you waxed inside her like a secret moon, she and I took long swaying walks every night after supper, brimming with tenderness and anxiety. By the short days of December, we began our walks after dark, so we kept to the lighted streets, not wanting to stumble. Mom was determined to hold out for the full nine months, which would end in January, because in that month Bloomington Hospital would begin allowing fathers into the delivery room, and she wanted me there. I was there, from the earliest pains right through your birth, holding her feverish hand, reminding her to take shallow breaths, mopping her forehead with a damp cloth, murmuring to her steadily all night, then babbling ecstatically when you arrived near dawn.

Nothing I had imagined beforehand prepared me for the sight of you, so perfectly made, so intent on life. Every inch of you pulsed with energy, hands groping, legs churning, and your skin glowed furnace red. I trembled. When your body convulsed for a gulp of our difficult air, I gasped. The sound of your first cry echoed through my bones. I wanted to shout. Maybe I did shout, because the nurses looked at me appraisingly, as if to calculate my need for a sedative. No matter how old this miracle, no matter how many times it has been repeated through the generations, it was brand new to me. You were the first baby ever born, my heart was sure of it. The birth of the universe could not have been more thrilling.

You were utterly fresh, every toe and finger and eyelash and cell an unprecedented wonder. Done up in a turquoise cap and gown like a refugee from an asylum, I sat in the hospital chair, my feet planted on the floor to make a solid lap, my back tense with responsibility, and for the first time I held you, so fearfully small, barely six pounds. My hands, cradling you, seemed clumsy and huge. Wondering, I bent down to feel your breath against my cheek. You smelled of apples. After a few minutes you started to whimper, so I handed you gingerly to Mom, knowing that only she could satisfy you. I stroked your fuzzy head while you nursed. How avidly you sucked, even before her milk began to flow. No monk in the rapture of meditation could have been more devoutly focused on God than you were on your mother's breast.

When it was time for you to go home, the nurse handed you to me while Mom lowered herself gingerly into a wheelchair. Only your drowsy eyes and tiny dollop of nose showed from an opening in the pink blanket—the inevitable pink blanket—in which you had been wrapped against the January cold. As I clutched you to my chest, a wave of worry swept over me. These experts in babies were actually going to let us take you out the door, as if we knew how to rear a child. What training had we ever had, except watching our own parents carelessly as we grew up? At least my watching had been haphazard; I can't speak for Mom's. Oh, sure, we'd read books on babies, but that's like reading manuals to learn about sex. It seemed outrageous, that a hospital would turn over a creature so tiny and precious and new to a pair of rank amateurs. Yet no one blocked our way as I pushed the wheelchair, with you in Mom's lap, down the tiled halls to the entrance, then out to our waiting car, its engine running and the heater on high. An orderly followed to fetch the chair. I half expected him to demand you back, but he only waved and wished us luck. I gave one lingering look at that haven of experts, and away we drove.

In early English, *wife* simply meant woman, as if a girl could not graduate to adulthood except by marrying. Farther back, *wife* sprang from an Indo-European root meaning to wrap, twist, or turn, a reference to the married woman's veil. To become a wife was to go into hiding from the world.

In most places and most ages where those words have been used, women were chattel, like any other piece of a man's property. Girls were betrothed at birth or in childhood, often married in adolescence, and married not for love but for the father's advantage—to return favors, forge alliances, settle disputes, clear debts, acquire land. Daughters were spendable coin. Once given or sold in marriage, the woman became a servant, if she was lucky, otherwise a concubine or slave.

Ancient history? During the week in which I begin this letter to you, dearest Eva, a puritanical faction has emerged victorious in the Afghan civil war. Their first act, after hanging the thugs who preceded them, was to order women off the streets, out of government, out of the professions, and back behind the veil. Any woman caught away from home with her face bare may be summarily whipped. Who would have thought, on the brink of the twenty-first century, that women could still be banished from public life, turned away from the light, wrapped up like packages to be opened only by husbands?

From the moment of your birth, every reference to women in the news, in literature, in jokes and jibes, took on for me a burning importance. I'd read the New Testament several times in childhood, but now suddenly I felt the menace in Paul's advice to Timothy: "Let a woman learn in silence with all submissiveness. I permit no woman to teach or to have authority over men; she is to keep silent. For Adam was formed first, then Eve; and Adam was not deceived, but the woman was deceived and became a transgressor." Suddenly I recognized the danger to women in the Genesis account of that primordial marriage—a "poetical story," as Mary Wollstonecraft called it, which certifies "that woman was created for man." Here was Eve, the original wife, created as an afterthought out of Adam's rib, giving in to the wily snake and her own appetite, plucking the apple, then foisting the forbidden fruit onto her innocent mate. This calumny against woman, the vain temptress, irked me all the more because her name is another form of yours, dear Eva, one that derives from the Hebrew word for life.

After blaming Eve for our fall from grace, Paul adds, "Yet woman will be saved through bearing children, if she continues in faith and love and holiness, with modesty." Paul reads Genesis selectively, of course, as patriarchs are inclined to do, ignoring the first version of the Creation, which grants Adam no priority: "So God created man in his own image, in the image of God he created him; male and female he created them. And God blessed them." *Them,* male and female. Jesus appealed to this earlier version when the Pharisees challenged him to see if he would approve of divorce: "Have you not read that he who made them from the beginning made them male and female, and said, 'For this reason a man shall leave his father and mother and be joined to his wife, and the two shall become one'? So they are no longer two but one. What therefore God has joined together, let no man put asunder."

Those words, in turn, have certainly caused much grief, forcing many couples to stay together in misery when they would have been far better off put asunder. Seen in historical context, however, Jesus' prohibition on divorce appears to be a stunning defense of women, for under the laws of Moses only men had the power to break a marriage. "For your hardness of heart," Jesus told the Pharisees, "Moses allowed you to divorce your wives, but from the beginning it was not so." That the abandoning of wives, especially those who failed to produce children, was an affliction in Israel might be surmised from repeated warnings in the Hebrew Bible. "Let none be faithless to the wife of his youth," Malachi insists. And the book of Proverbs offers these instructions to Jewish men:

> Let your fountain be blessed,
> and rejoice in the wife of your youth,
> a lovely hind, a graceful doe.
> Let her affection fill you at all times with delight,
> be infatuated always with her love.

Paul certainly honored love and loyalty in marriage, but not equality. In one of the more notorious passages from his letters, he proclaims: "Wives, be subject to your husbands, as to the Lord. For the husband is the head of the wife as Christ is the head of the church, his body, and is himself its Savior. As the church is subject to Christ, so let wives also be subject in everything to their husbands."

Again, this is not ancient history I'm rehearsing. Paul's words, together with those of Moses and countless other patriarchs through the ages, still influence the prospects for women today. Those who hold power never give it up without a fight. Only recently, Pope Paul VI reaffirmed that women may not become priests within the Catholic Church ("I permit no woman to teach or to have authority over men; she is to keep silent.") and that birth control is a sin ("Yet woman will be saved through bearing children."). Well, I set myself against those ancient prejudices. I oppose any constraints that apply only to women, and my concern for you and your fate adds to the warmth of my opposition.

Multiply this little excursion of thought by a million, and you will begin to see how your birth made the reputation and condition of women *personal* for me. Statistics on rape, on poverty, on wife-beating, on single mothers, on jobs and pay for women became disturbing facts about the society in which my daughter would grow up. Would you be injured by the sexual fantasies pumped out endlessly by advertisers and filmmakers and rock stars and cranks? Would you be free to pursue your talents, wherever they might lead? Whenever I learned of women being hurt or ridiculed or held back, I thought immediately of you. Would you be scarred or scorned? Would you find men blocking your path, soldiers or bureaucrats or executives? And how was I implicated in the shameful history of men mistreating women?

Even falling in love with the woman who would become your mother had not inspired in me such troubled questioning, because she was brilliant in science, in music, in writing and speech; she was poised and confident; she balanced on her own center. She had found a husband with plenty of flaws, but one who would never lay a hand on her except in love, never betray or desert her. To my bedazzled eyes, this Ruth Ann McClure seemed to have emerged into womanhood unscathed. But you were just beginning. How would you fare? Loving you, wishing you a full and free and joyous life, I set about pondering the lives of women as I never had in all the years before your birth.

On hearing that we'd had a baby, many of our friends and acquaintances, women as well as men, asked first of all: "What is it?" I was sorely tempted to answer, "Human," yet I knew what they meant, of course. So I played along, saying, "She's a girl, a hungry, fidgety, wonderful girl." Only then did they ask your name, your weight, the color of your eyes and hair, and how the delivery had gone.

Among the books we read while preparing nervously for your arrival were several on gender bias in child rearing. The pink and blue treatment begins early, we learned. Studies of delivery rooms show that nurses tend to handle boys more roughly and speak to them more loudly. Mothers of newborns often carry on these distinctions, holding girls closely and gently, holding boys loosely and distantly, murmuring to the girls and talking firmly to the boys. So from the outset, the paths begin to fork, and for a child nudged in one direction or the other, there may be no going back. In videotaped experiments, mothers presented with toddlers whom they do not know tend to be more verbal and soothing with those dressed as girls, gruffer and more physical with those dressed as boys; they keep the girls close by, within easy reach, while they encourage the boys to move out and explore the room. Supplied with an array of toys, these mothers will usually offer trucks and balls and hammers to the infants they take to be boys, and will offer dolls, mirrors, and dress-up clothes to the ones they take to be girls. I suspect that fathers might have acted in similar ways, but the experiments appear never to have included fathers, perhaps because the men were busy driving trucks and swinging hammers and roving about.

Reading all of that before your birth, and not yet realizing how stubborn human character and culture are, your mother and I vowed to resist these warping influences. We would rear you purely as a child, neither girl nor boy, so that you might grow like a tree in full sunlight, taking on your own natural shape. You arrived early in 1973, after all, a time when many of us who were under thirty considered nature to be all-wise and culture to be a snarl of rusty chains, easily broken. We would seek out playmates for you whose parents were also striving to break the old gender shackles. We would allow into our house only those books, magazines, television programs, and visitors that honored your right to become whatever your heart and mind led you to be. We would put before you the whole rainbow of human possibilities, and let you choose.

Yet there you were, two days old, riding home from the hospital swaddled in a pink blanket. It was a gift from someone so close to us that we could not say no, the first of many such gifts. Clearly, whatever Mom and I might decide about rearing you, the world would have its say, right from the beginning, and the world's say would grow louder each year.

By the time I carried you into the house, presents had already begun to accumulate there in drifts, most of them cuddly, frilly, and pastel. Enough dolls to start a nursery, a teddy bear that mooed when it rolled over, a robin's-egg-blue satin pillow with a music box inside that played a Brahms lullaby, morally uplifting storybooks, pale baby duds for every occasion, and soft mobiles to dangle over your crib. I didn't rush out and buy you a GI Joe and miniature chain saw and baseball glove to even things up. But I did make sure you had a toolbox fitted with toy hammer and screwdriver and wrench, and a board rigged out with plastic hinges and bells and gears, and a little bench for pounding. Thus, I began smuggling into your life my own hopes for who you might turn out to be.

Try as we might, Mom and I could not shield you from everything the world expected of girls, least of all from the expectations buried deep in ourselves. We could not undo our own upbringing, could not erase the hundreds of films and thousands of books and millions of images we'd taken in. Each of us had built up a composite notion of maleness and femaleness from all the boys and girls, men and women we had met, beginning with our own parents. Even though we wrestled with those notions, trying to break their hold, they still left their marks on us, visible and invisible. When we cuddled you, spoke to you, played and romped and dreamed with you, who could say what unconscious impulses reached you through our hands and lips?

You certainly kept our hands and lips and every other bit of us occupied in those early months. For the first year or so, you rarely slept more than two or three hours at a stretch, and never through the whole night. Although I must have been tired, the weariness has washed out of memory, and now I remember only the bliss of watching you, tracing the weather of your face; I remember feeding you the one nightly bottle that gave Mom relief from nursing; I remember bathing you in the sink, with a towel underneath to shield you from the chilly porcelain; I remember rocking you, or flying you around the room at arm's length, or spinning a leaf in front of your face so it tickled your nose, or showing you snow. I remember carrying you for hours each night as I paced around the apartment, and soothing you with songs. As soon as you found your voice, you began to sing along, in a skittery language known only to babies and sleepless parents. When I exhausted the repertoire that I could remember from my own father's singing, I worked my way through anthologies of folk songs, from immigrant ballads through whaling chanteys and spirituals and lullabies and love ditties and blues, skipping only those selections that featured bloodshed, drugs, or booze.

You've heard most of these memories before, even read some of them in my books, for I never tire of talking about you. When I sit down to make this small present of words for your wedding, I can't help recalling the child you were behind the woman you've become. There wouldn't be paper enough to hold all the memories of your growing up, so I recount only a few from the early years, when your character took shape.

In your very first spring, one blustery March day I was carrying you, bundled in a blanket, along the sidewalk from house to car. Before I reached the street, you stiffened in my arms, twisted your face about, and gazed with a startled look into the empty air. I stopped, looked around, but could not figure out what had provoked you. "What's up, kiddo?" I asked. You weren't saying. I snugged the blanket around you and took another step. Again you jerked, swiveled your head, stared. Only then did I feel what you were feeling—the breath of March. My eyes flared wide, and my face turned into the amazing wind.

Later that same spring, I was pushing you in the stroller one afternoon when you noticed a peach-pit moon near the horizon. You reached for it, fingers splayed, and started fussing when you discovered that your arm wasn't long enough. "That's the moon," I told you, "and it's far, far away." Months later, when you were just beginning to put sentences together, once again we came upon a ghostly moon during a walk, and this time you announced, "There's the moon. Want it, Daddy." Even if your arm wasn't long enough to reach it, you figured, then surely mine would be. I had to disappoint you, of course, and also to disappoint myself, because your hunger for the moon revived my own.

Again and again, your frank wonder stripped away the glaze of familiarity from the world. Look at that fiery ball in the sky! Smell that dirt! Taste that good water going down! Feel those wavy lines in wood! When it stormed, you and I would sit on the porch in a rocker, the rumble of thunder and sizzle of rain in our ears, mist on our faces, as still as we could be. When the leaves fell, we raked up heaps in the backyard and you plowed through them, grabbing and flinging, nibbling, yelping. What a universe! What a life! Was there no end to the surprises? You squatted tirelessly to study bees nuzzling the throats of flowers. You gawked at butterflies as they tilted overhead, spinning around until you grew dizzy. You rushed from firefly to firefly as they simmered in the grass. Anything living would captivate you—a dog, a cat, a spider, a roly-poly on the windowsill, a blue jay scrawking in the maple tree, a fern breaking ground, another child toddling along, a grown-up's idly jostling foot. How exactly right that a girl who stopped in her tracks whenever she spied a bird, who fed bread to ducks and swans, who picked up every feather she found, who tilted her face skyward in spring and fall when the geese went honking by—that such a girl should grow up to become a biologist and study birds.

As birds seem to embody your love of air, so whales seem to embody your love of water. That affection, too, began early on. You first met the ocean at Little Boars Head beach in New Hampshire, when you were eighteen months old, squealing with surprise as the waves licked your bare feet. On our return trips to

New England, up and down the coast from Cape Cod to Maine, you dipped in the chilly Atlantic or rode in boats on its choppy waters. You would stare at the surf with the same focused eagerness that you once showed when nursing, and with the same reluctance to break away. You were five when you met the Pacific, at Heceta Beach, near Florence, Oregon. You clambered through a maze of driftwood logs, lurked around tide pools, stood watching waves break on rock. From a bluff on that same coast you saw your first whales, California grays migrating north, and ever after you took these great creatures to be the soul of the sea. For years, whenever anyone asked what you hoped to do when you grew up, you would answer, "Study whales."

The whales eventually swam away from the center of your imagination, but the ocean remained. Clearly, though you were born and bred a midwestern girl, and though you've come back here to the landlocked heart of the continent to study and get married, some deep part of you hungers for the sea. Or perhaps what you hunger for is not so much the vastness of ocean as the force of moving water. From your earliest days, you've been drawn to the roar of rain, the flow of rivers, the tumble of falls, the sluice of snowmelt in the street. You may have caught some of that passion from me, but not all of it. During the year we spent in Exeter, when you turned two, our favorite destination for walks was the bridge over the Squamscott River where the old mill stood. You would gaze down from one side of the bridge at the tumbling water for a long while, then take my hand and cross the street to gaze down from the other side. No matter what your mood when we set out, after a few minutes at the river, you would grow calm and clear and gathered, and so would I.

In contrast to that serenity, your other dominant mood has

always been a fierce whirl of energy, finely controlled. You began gymnastics and dancing the same year that you first spied whales. In our rented house, you would race full tilt down the hallway, plant your hands on the arm of the couch, and go vaulting over onto the cushions. On the springy grass of the backyard, you turned endless cartwheels and flips, asking me to spot you on the tricky ones. At the ballet studio you began the long training that would one day send you gliding down the aisle with a dancer's grace. There was nothing delicate or fragile about you when you leapt and turned, but rather a dazzling strength, akin to the strength of wind blowing and water flowing and wild creatures moving freely. What are birds, after all, but the most accomplished dancers, who can maneuver in thin air?

Whether in motion or still, you've always been a rapt observer. From the beginning, we took you with us when we visited friends, and you would sit in the midst of the grown-ups with saucer eyes and avid ears. At bedtime, no matter whose house we happened to be in, we could lay you down on a blanket on the floor of a nearby room, and you would go to sleep without a peep. That was the price you paid for getting to tag along and overhear adult conversation. Although you had lots to say when you were alone with Mom or me, in company you preferred to listen and watch.

That is the essence of what you do now, as a scientist, listening and watching. Only now, instead of a roomful of grown-ups, what fascinates you is an aviary full of birds, or a field thick with grasses and insects, or a river churning with otters, or a notebook full of data. You have a head for discovering patterns, and a heart for loving them.

So do I, darling Eva, although the patterns I care about are made mostly of language and memory. To a surprising degree, marriage is made of the same ingredients. You begin, if you're lucky, with a rush of romance, but you continue at the slower pace of shared history, a history that stays with you in stories, habits, recipes, photographs, clothes, art on the walls, rumpled sofas, potted plants, and, just maybe, in children. The two of you talk. You touch. You reminisce. You plan. You cook and clean and cope. Together you weave a fabric that neither of you could have made alone. The strength of that fabric depends on circumstances beyond your control, of course, but also on the care and patience and commitment you bring to the effort.

I started out this rambling letter by recalling your birth, because a wedding is a birth of another sort. In becoming husband and wife, a man and woman do not cease to be individuals, yet they become in addition someone new, a compound self. Two shall become one, as Jesus said. Maybe in this paradox there is something of what twins experience, each one distinct and yet each one dwelling in constant awareness of the other. Living with a mate is harder than living alone, but also richer. No learning in my life has been more difficult, humbling, or surprising than the daily lessons of marriage. As you begin your own marriage, I want you to know that I still rejoice in the wife of my youth. After thirty years, I am still infatuated with her love. I don't count this fidelity as a virtue of mine or hers, but as a great and enduring gift.

Since I held you on your first day of life, dearest Eva, I have been fretting about the cruel and belittling images of women that circulate out there in the big, bad world. I would erase them all if

I had the power. And while I was making the world safer for you, I would work a few changes on men as well. The prospect of your wedding has made me worry afresh about my half of the species, with our penchant for selfishness and surliness, our insecurities, our aimless hungers, and our yen for power. I keep reminding myself that you are not marrying men in general but only one man, and quite a good one. My wish for your marriage is that you and Matthew may fashion your own history of shared work, talk, music, nourishing meals, memorable journeys, fine friends, mutual aid and respect and joy. Being married is a life's work, as demanding and rewarding as anything you will ever do.

To Jesse, on Your Marriage

After you and Carrie Dean have set up house in Chicago, surrounded by all the bowls and blankets and bijoux offered by friends at your wedding, maybe these bare words from me will seem like an odd sort of gift. You can't eat words, can't wear them, can't stretch them over your heads to keep off rain. Yet I wanted to make a small present with my own hands, something not for sale in stores. So I write you this letter.

Your hands are now larger than mine, more skilled in cooking and guitar playing, but when I saw them first, as you lay in your mother's arms on the birthing table, they were balled into fists the size of walnuts, and they knew only how to grab and cling. You arrived at five-thirty in the morning after a short labor, your head emerging first with a damp crown of ginger hair. Your eyes, slate gray, opened wide to stare at the faces looming over you. Like any baby, at the start you were little more than a bundle of hungers, fierce and fragile at the same time. You needed those doctors and nurses to help usher you into the world, needed your mother to feed and fondle you, soon even needed me to soothe you to sleep.

Already having a daughter whom I loved immoderately, I wondered how I would feel toward a son. As I imagined things back then, a daughter is born into the world free of the past, a child making a fresh start. A son, though, is born carrying on his shoulders the history of men's mistreatment of women. Although he is innocent of those past deeds, a boy will be called to account for this troubling legacy, in the way every white person born in America must answer for slavery and every Gentile born in Germany must answer for the Holocaust.

A father will also be called to account for the sort of man his son becomes. I knew that being father to a son would differ from being father to a daughter, but I didn't know how. I understood that I would become a model for you—to imitate or reject—whether I wished it so or not. In rearing you, I have had to examine my own life, have had to think back through my father and grandfathers and all the men who've shaped me. Which is to say, I didn't fully become a son until I had one of my own. Fathers are often accused of being overly protective of their daughters, and that may be true of me, but it's equally true that ever since your birth I've wanted to safeguard you. I've tried to shield you from harm, even while realizing I can't always succeed.

During your first few years, I often retrieved you from the crib when you were crying, loaded you into the backpack, and took you out for walks. In the daytime, you would babble while I sang or told stories; at night you rode in silence, wide awake, gazing up at the stars. You cut your first tooth one night in Yellowstone Park as we camped on our way west, and so to spare your mother and sister and our neighbors in the campground from your wailing, I carried you outside under the full moon. With you in the pack, the two of us cast a humpbacked moon shadow, and the soft light made the stony land seem tender. Although you quickly hushed your crying, I could tell you were awake from the shifting of your body and from the grip of your hands in my beard. Even now, as I think of such walks, I can feel the weight and warmth of you against me.

Now, twenty-two years after your birth, when you stop by our house to run a load of laundry or share a meal, when you tell me about your college studies, deal with your pile of mail, or borrow a tool to fix your car, I can't help feeling astonished by the speed with which that teething infant became this skillful man. Your hands, which once could not tie a shoe, can now program a computer or filet a fish. Your mind, which once could not add three fingers plus three to make six, can now follow the convolutions of calculus. In little more than two decades, you've mastered much of what humans have taken millennia to invent or discover, from the speaking and writing of our lush language to the balancing of a spreadsheet. Every healthy child, with help from parents and teachers, achieves miracles of learning, but that does not make the transformation any less amazing.

I don't know how to convey the wonder I feel on meeting in you a separate mind. How did this consciousness arise? It is neither mine nor your mother's; it is a wholly new presence in the world. My own thoughts are so familiar to me that I take them for granted, forgetting how strange it is that matter should think. In you, however, I have watched a mind grow from nothing to a formidable power. As an infant, you did little besides eat and sleep. Soon came spells when you would lie quietly in the crib, fiddling with your toes or listening to a lullaby or watching a mobile, and there would appear in your eyes the dazed look of discovery, as if the impressions pouring into you from all sides were beginning to bounce around in your skull. Not long after you learned to speak, you proclaimed your independence by saying "No!" with a show of glee. You began asking questions insatiably, as if life were a grand puzzle that you and you alone had been sent here to solve. You sensed a fabulous power in grasshoppers and grass, in starfish and stars, in the splayed fingers of your own hand. As you grew up, just as you learned to stand on your own feet and run on your own legs, so you came to think more and more for yourself. Now, in your twenty-third year, your mind has become a cosmos of knowledge, imagination, and memory.

One does not give a son away in marriage as fathers traditionally give away daughters. The groom is understood to be his own master, to possess himself. And yet a son is the offspring of a family, the fruit of a community, shaped by many teachers, so he carries in his skin far more than his own weight.

The roots of *husband* are those for the words *house* and *bound*. If a bachelor is a man who's footloose and fancy-free, able to flit among women like a bee among flowers, a husband is a man who has quit wandering, a man who has settled down in one place with one woman. A bachelor can remain a boy if he wishes, following his own desires wherever they might lead. A husband must grow up, learning to braid his desires together with those of his wife.

It's no surprise that men joke about marriage as a ball and chain, as if by joining yourself to a woman you sink into bondage. True, you give up certain liberties when you vow to love, honor, and cherish another human being for the rest of your days. But I have found marriage to be the trading of a cheap kind of freedom for a richer and more durable kind. My own marriage has nourished and steadied me. It has not kept me from admiring other women, has not kept me from venturing into the world, has not dimmed my own peculiar light. On the contrary, by providing me with an emotional center, marriage has allowed me to appreciate other women without possessing them, to journey outward from a home base, to become more fully myself.

If lifelong fidelity between a man and a woman came easily, we would not need to shore it up with the ceremony of marriage. The witnesses who look on from the pews are there not only to share the joy of the newlyweds but also to help them feel the weight of their vows. I remember feeling sobered in the midst of my wedding, when I gazed across at the woman who would become your mother and I promised to join myself with her through sickness as well as health, through sorrow and joy, right up until death should part us. In all my life up to that moment I had never made such a huge commitment, nor have I made any since that would rival it, except in becoming a father.

I took no vow of love when you were born. I never stood before a congregation to promise that I would honor and cherish you, that I would care for you no matter what you might need so long as I breathed. The mere sight of your ginger hair and slate-gray eyes emerging from the woman I love forced me to love you as well. I say *forced* because the claim you made on me from the beginning was sharp and total. Whether I wished to or not, I found myself longing night and day for your health and happiness.

When you were an infant, your needs were so simple that all they cost me were a little sleep and a lot of patience. As the years passed, however, your needs grew more complex, along with the puzzling cosmos of your mind. There came a time when you begged for clothes or toys like those owned by your friends at school. Soon you began to reel from the charms of girls, who could pitch you high or low in the length of a phone call. Then you needed to fill your room with a roaring surf of music, night and day, to soothe your frazzled nerves. Before long you decided your life would be ruined unless you had the daily use of a car. By the time you were sixteen and seventeen, it seemed that nothing I did, nothing I stood for, could satisfy you. No gift of words or time, no offering of patience or sleep, could please you.

So we began to pay for being father and son in the coin of heartache and anger. We shouted at one another. We slammed doors. Remember, when our quarrels were at their worst, how we took long walks to cool our tempers? It would have been easier for us to turn our backs on one another, go stomping off in opposite directions to brood and fume. Instead, I would tell you we needed to go for a walk. You'd be reluctant, insisting you had nothing more to say, but after a while you'd pull on your boots and we'd set off. Usually, for the first few blocks you said nothing, even when I asked you questions. But gradually you began to speak, and soon you were pouring out your worry and anger, your stream of accusations. Now and again I answered with accusations of my own, but mainly I listened, trying to hear to the depths of your hurt. Our voices began loud, then slowly dwindled, until we might have appeared like two friends out for a stroll. We walked sometime for hours, miles and miles around Bloomington, and in the evenings the lights in houses would go out one after another, and we might return after midnight. Even if those walks did not bring peace between us, they did keep us talking and listening. They reminded us that our love for one another is deeper and stronger than any of our differences. And that is an essential fact about any lasting friendship, whether between father and son or between husband and wife.

It was because of my love that I kept setting limits for you, even when the quickest way to bring harmony would have been to let you do whatever you wanted. I realized then that you needed my resistance to push against, to test your strength, to define yourself. So you kept turning up the volume of your stereo until I asked you to turn it down, you kept staying out later until I set a firm hour when you had to be home, you kept driving faster until I resolved to take away the keys. Mother helped set those limits, of course, but I was the one who called you to account. The drawing of those boundaries was my way of reminding you that none of us lives alone in the world, that our actions—including the risks we take—affect other people, especially those who love us the most.

In spite of those limits, we gave you as much freedom as you would responsibly use. You began traveling on your own to distant places at an age when my own parents would not have let me drive by myself to the next county. You saw more of the world before you finished high school than I had seen before I turned forty. You grew up swiftly during high school, maybe too swiftly, because so many of your friends suffered grown-up griefs. I remember that one friend was raped; one lost her mother to cancer, another lost his father; some spiraled down into drink or drugs; a few discovered they were homosexual and opened themselves to scorn; several grew so furious with parents that they moved out to live on their own; several watched their parents fly apart into divorce; some got pregnant; one ran away.

As a teenager, you often said that I couldn't possibly understand you, because you had seen so much more of life than I had at your age. There may have been some truth in that claim, although you made it in ignorance of what I had lived through. It was easy to imagine that I had always been a middle-aged professor with a desk full of paperwork and a calendar full of chores. True, at your age, I hadn't worried about drugs or AIDS, but I had seen girls drop out of my class to bear fatherless children, had seen a child wither from leukemia, had watched a grandfather spiral down into dementia, had grieved with schoolmates over the death of a mother or father, had lost friends to drink and war. Loss taught me to relish whatever endured—art and music and science, literature and language, good work, the sun and moon, the green earth—and loss taught me to celebrate the gift of my own brief life.

By the time you graduated from high school, the tension between us had begun to ease. Our camping trips into the Rockies, Smokies, and Canyonlands helped us find the language to speak of our shared affections. In such wild places, in the presence of such vast powers, our struggles seemed petty and tame. Gradually, with ever-growing trust between us, we began to talk in ways that my own father and I had never talked—about God and books, about money and morals, about our hopes and fears, about the matters close to our hearts. My father and I talked only about sports, animals, and trees, about the weather or the headlines. You and I have talked about those things as well, but we have also gone deeper. My father had the intelligence and insight to go anywhere in conversation I could have gone, but he chose to stay on the surface, as if he feared that by diving into the depths we might drown. I've swum in the depths with you, and I've risen back into the daylight feeling stronger for having faced the pressure, feeling grateful to you for traveling with me.

We used to mark your height every few months on the door casing in the kitchen, showing your explosive growth as you overtook your mother, then your sister, then me. As you grew, increasingly I turned to you whenever there was heavy work to do, not only because I needed help but also because I delighted in your strength. So you and I dug up the garden, split wood for the stove, pounded nails, carried furniture and stones. Maybe the hardest we ever worked together was this past summer, when we demolished the old hippie A-frame, taking it apart shingle by shingle, board by board, with hammers and crowbars and our gloved hands. The labor took us nearly six weeks, during a record heat wave that caused several hundred deaths in the Midwest alone. We drank water every half-hour, but still in an afternoon each of us would lose three or four pounds. That was astonishing to me, since I could remember when you weighed little more than four pounds. And here, as we worked in the terrible heat, I could see your muscles bulge, I could watch the sweat trickle down through the rusty beard on your chin, I could talk with you about politics and philosophy.

In one of the photos I keep in the gallery on my writing desk, taken when you were two, I hold you in my lap as I sit on the ground with my back against the trunk of the big elm in our front yard. Each of us wears blue jeans and a plaid flannel shirt. Both pairs of jeans are white about the knees from the crawling we've been doing as we play games on the living room floor. My forehead is creased and my eyes glint from shadowy sockets, while your eyes, long since turned from slate gray to brown, are squeezed nearly shut by the pressure of your smile, and your bright face is as plump and smooth as risen dough. Your head tilts back against my chest and your blond hair gleams in the sunlight. My hair is still thick, long about the ears, and dark brown, and I'm still wearing a beard. By age two you knew better than to reach up and tug on that beard when you wanted my attention. In this photograph, you press your hands against your belly as if you're holding in a laugh, and one of my hands curls over yours. We both grin at the person who's holding the camera, your mother and my wife. She has caught us in a moment of radiant joy.

Beside that picture I keep another one, taken last August during our kayaking trip in Glacier Bay. Along one of the stony beaches, you and Carrie Dean are sitting close together on a drift log, faces touching cheek-to-cheek, your arms wrapped around her. Instead of being held, as you were in the earlier photo, now you're the one doing the holding. You're a larger man here than I was when I cradled you in my lap; you must weigh ten times as much as you did at age two. Your hair, still ginger, is tousled by wind, and your eyes are squinted up against the sun. In the background, sun licks a pale green band of rye grass and a dark green band of alder trees. You and Carrie Dean fill the foreground with the brightness of your smiles. You announced your engagement a few days before we left for Glacier Bay, and in this photograph the two of you are jubilant over the prospect of marriage.

As I sit here making this gift of words for your wedding, my eyes keep moving from one photograph to the other, and my mind keeps moving between memories of you as a child and impressions of you as a grown man. As I think about your becoming a husband and maybe in time a father, I can't help revisiting all the ages you've passed through. By marrying, you prepare a space where children of your own may appear one day, to sit in your lap and swiftly grow up and then perhaps to marry. If children do appear in that space, then you'll have a chance to feel astonished by their swift change from infant to adult.

May you and Carrie Dean savor marriage, Jesse, as I have done these many years. Blessings on you both.

Hawk Rising

I've known red-tailed hawks my whole life, spying their hunched silhouettes on poles and bare trees, their husky shapes wheeling in the sky, from the Great Lakes to the Gulf of Mexico, from the rocky margins of Maine to the coast of Oregon, and along the highways and fencerows and pastures in between. But I had never fully *seen* a redtail until a few years ago, during a visit to my childhood place in Ohio after my father's death. I was walking the familiar land, brooding on things lost, when a great hawk launched out from a branch over my head and loosed its piercing cry, and I looked up to see the bird swerving in the air, and I knew it was my father.

I don't mean it looked like my vanished father. It looked like a classic eastern redtail—creamy underneath with a scattering of dark feathers across the belly, black strokes along the front edges and tips of the wings, the famous ruddy tail splayed in the sun—but it *felt* like my father. And I felt for a few heartbeats like the son of that soaring bird, like the offspring of a hawk. I sensed the tug of rising air, glimpsed the rumpled quilt of woodlots and fields spread out to the horizon. For those few moments I rode the wind.

The spell soon passed. I recalled my clumsy human shape, the dirt beneath my boots, the weight of my limbs. Yet the distance that opened once more between the hawk and me was not the same as it had been before our meeting. The bird soared away beyond the reach of my vision, but it remained my father. I was left realizing a kinship for which I had no language.

I've spent several years now trying to figure out what to make of this experience. Whatever the source of my feeling of kinship, whether it arose from grief or nostalgia or plain confusion, the feeling itself was real, as undeniable as a stone held in the hand. Whatever the truth of that bewildering encounter, it changed the way I see. I can't hike the hills near my home in southern Indiana, can't drive across country, can't visit deserts or parks without looking for red-tailed hawks. I can't meet anyone who spends time outdoors without asking for news of them. I talk with falconers who train them, farmers who shoot them, rehabilitators who mend their wings. I read everything I can find about these hawks, study them in photographs and films and occasionally on a handler's gloved fist.

I have learned that the redtail is not only a champion at soaring, riding thermals for hours at a time, it can also hover by flapping, the way kestrels do, and it can hang in one spot on extended wings, as though leaning into the wind, a maneuver known as kiting. The redtail doesn't often take prey from the sky; it usually swoops down from a perch. Farmers used to call it the hen hawk, because it will sometimes claim a chicken. More commonly the redtail eats voles, mice, frogs, lizards, crabs, prairie dogs, muskrats, squirrels, grasshoppers, pigeons and smaller birds. It's a celebrated killer of snakes. Among the thirty-odd American birds of prey, only the kestrel rivals it for adaptability, as the redtail ranges from the edge of tree line in Alaska to Central America and the West Indies, from tundra to desert. In the desert it may nest in a saguaro cactus, but in wooded country it builds a nest of sticks high in a tree, sometimes adding sprigs of evergreen. A pair will defend the nest against all intruders, including human ones, and during the breeding season they will guard a hunting territory that may be several square miles. Redtails court in January and February, and during the spring, mates can often be seen perched side by side, the larger female and smaller male, sometimes with shoulders touching. The pair remains together until the fledglings scatter in August or September; then the male and female go their separate ways until the following year, when they mate once more.

You'll recognize my obsession with red-tailed hawks if you've ever been fascinated by a bird or a beast. For a two-legged animal to become obsessed with creatures that move about on two wings—or on four legs, for that matter, or fishy fins, or on a belly of scaly skin—is far from rare, but it's nonetheless mysterious. How strange that so many of us devote ourselves to studying or defending other species that we have no desire to eat, own, or control. I have in mind not only the advocates for whooping cranes or wolves, for monarch butterflies, grizzly bears, bull trout, or the countless other species imperiled by our sprawling way of life. I think also of those who cherish the abundant garden-variety creatures. I think of the man who traces the trails of ants, the woman who charts the work of beavers in her creek, the child who builds nesting boxes for bluebirds and keeps track of the chicks. I think of all those who pay attention to other species with the passion and devotion that we usually reserve for the people we love.

What inspires these attachments? The biologist Edward O.

Wilson has given us a useful word, *biophilia,* for our innate attraction to other forms of life. The feeling of kinship that I'm puzzling about may only be a special case of biophilia, an intensification of this alertness toward anything in our vicinity that moves and breathes. But even if the passionate curiosity about other species is rooted in our evolutionary need to eat and avoid being eaten, if carried far enough it enlarges our sense of who we are, where we are, and how we might live.

When my daughter was in grade school, one of her classmates often brought snakes to class in his lunch box. Every now and again he would open the box and stare inside, barely blinking. Why was he so nuts about snakes, my daughter asked the boy. Because they go places I can't go, he answered. They know things I don't know. He was mesmerized by snakiness, by this cool, coiled, contemplative way of being. The boy has grown up to become a breeder of reptiles and an advocate for their protection. I'm convinced that his infatuation with snakes, however it began, has endured because it gives him a wider view of life.

I have known children and adults who've been mesmerized by crayfish or catfish, water striders or warblers, by swallow-tailed butterflies or white-tailed deer, by coyotes or crickets or crows. When these enthusiasts talk about their cherished creatures, a wonder comes into their voices. They tell of astounding migrations, exquisite adaptations, perceptions far beyond our ken. They speak with the excitement of messengers bringing news from foreign tribes. Look at these other ways of dwelling in the world, they tell us, each way elegant and instructive.

And isn't that what we long for, a reassurance that we aren't alone in this feverish business of breeding and dying? We yearn not merely to survive from moment to moment, but to live more abundantly, more variously, more richly. Our dilemma as a species is that we have no clear and confident way of being—we must figure out how to be human, how to behave, and we are in constant danger of forgetting. But that dilemma is also our gift, because it invites us to reach out to other species and learn what we can of their ways.

Long-settled peoples everywhere have studied their durable neighbors, pondering raven or frog, grizzly or salmon, lion or kangaroo. In our own young and clumsy culture, so noisy with the buzz of human doings, we've been slow to acknowledge these parallel lives. Yet even in suburbs and cities, if we look and listen, other species may claim our attention, not necessarily in one blazing moment, as when the hawk laid claim to me, but perhaps over months or years. Slowly or quickly, we begin to notice creatures we had scarcely noticed before. A familiar animal ceases to be an object and becomes a subject, with its own fascinating inwardness, and thereby deserving of our compassion and care.

For all our faults as a species—and we have our share—this capacity to see other creatures not as rivals nor prey but as fellow beings worthy of wonder and respect is surely a redeeming trait. By recognizing our affiliation with hawk or wolf or moth, we fill more than our bellies, save more than our skins. Paradoxically, we might be most fully human when we go out of ourselves, tracing our kinship with fellow travelers that leap and lope and crawl and fly.

A Shawnee man once heard me describing my encounter with the red-tailed hawk. When I spoke of the hawk as my father, the man leaned over to a mutual friend and whispered, "He's Indian." What he meant, the friend later told me, is that within the Shawnee tradition it is perfectly natural to recognize such a kinship between a dead ancestor and a living animal.

Such a discovery is much harder to fit into my own broadly scientific tradition. I don't want to play Indian. But I must make room for my experience. Although science teaches me that I am kin to other species, that we all belong to one great genetic family, that my arm and a bird's wing evolved from the same ancestral forms, science does not give me the language to say that the hawk is my father. That lesson came from the hawk itself. The redtail convinced me of my kinship, no longer merely as an intellectual notion derived from the study of biology, but now as a truth of the heart.

Now, even when the sky is empty, I carry the bird inside me. I bear some sense of its hunger, its drive to reproduce, its need for hunting space, its keen gaze. Any time I pause to think of it I can watch it soar. The hawk rises, tilts on the subtleties of air, and keeps on rising.

Silence

Finding a traditional Quaker meeting in Indianapolis would not be easy. No steeple would loom above the meetinghouse, no bell tower, no neon cross. No billboard out front would name the preacher or proclaim the sermon topic or tell sinners how to save their souls. No crowd of nattily dressed churchgoers would stream toward the entrance from a vast parking lot filled with late-model cars. No bleat and moan of organ music would roll from the sanctuary doors.

I knew all of that from having worshiped with Quakers off and on for thirty years, beginning when I was a graduate student in England. They are a people who call so little attention to themselves or their gathering places as to be nearly invisible. Yet when I happened to be in Indianapolis one Sunday this past January, I still set out in search of the meetinghouse without street address or map. My search was not made any easier by the snow lolling down on the city that morning. I recalled hearing that the North Meadow Circle of Friends gathers in a house near the intersection of Meridian and Sixteenth Streets, a spot I found easily enough. Although I could not miss the imposing Catholic Center nearby on Meridian, nor the Joy of All Who Sorrow Eastern Orthodox Church just a block away on Sixteenth, the only landmark at the intersection itself was the International House of Pancakes. Figuring somebody in there might be able to direct me to the Quakers, I went inside, where I was greeted by the smell of sausage and the frazzled gaze of the hostess. No, she'd never heard of any Quakers.

"But there's the phone book," she told me, gesturing with a sheaf of menus. "You're welcome to look them up."

I thanked her, and started with the yellow pages. No luck under "Churches." Nothing under "Religion." Nothing under "Quakers" or "Friends, Society of." Finally, in the white pages, I found a listing for the North Meadow Circle, with a street address just a couple of blocks away.

As I returned the phone book to its cubbyhole, I glanced across the room, where a throng of diners tucked into heaping platters of food, and I saw through the plate-glass window a man slouching past on the sidewalk. He wore a knit hat encrusted with leaves, a jacket torn at the elbows to reveal several dingy layers of cloth underneath, baggy trousers held up with a belt of rope, and broken leather shoes wrapped with silver duct tape. His face was the color of dust. He carried a bulging gray sack over his shoulder, like a grim Santa Claus. Pausing at a trash can, he bent down to retrieve something, stuffed the prize in his bag, then shuffled north on Meridian into the slant of snow.

I thought how odd it was that none of the diners rushed out to drag him from the street into the House of Pancakes for a hot meal. Then again, I didn't rush out either. I only stood there feeling pangs of guilt, an ache as familiar as heartburn. What held me back? Wouldn't the Jesus whom I try to follow in my own muddled way have chosen to feed that man instead of searching for a prayer meeting? I puzzled over this as I drove the few blocks to Talbott Street, on the lookout for number 1710, the address I had turned up in the phone book. The root of all my reasons for neglecting that homeless man, I decided, was fear. He might be crazy, might be strung out, might be dangerous. He would almost certainly have problems greater than I could solve. And there were so many more like him, huddled out front of missions or curled up in doorways all over Indianapolis this bitterly cold morning. If I fed one person, why not two? Why not twenty? Once I acknowledged the human need rising around me, what would keep me from drowning in all that hurt?

A whirl of guilt and snow blinded me to number 1710, even though I cruised up and down that stretch of Talbott Street three times. I did notice that the neighborhood was in transition, with some houses boarded up and others newly spiffed up. A few of the homes were small enough for single families, but most were big frame duplexes trimmed in fretwork and painted in pastels, or low brick apartment buildings that looked damp and dark and cheap. On my third pass along Talbott I saw a portly man with a bundle of papers clamped under one arm turning in at the gate of a gray clapboard house. I rolled down my window to ask if he knew where the Friends worshiped, and he answered with a smile, "Right here."

I parked nearby in a lot belonging to the Herron School of Art. As I climbed out of the car, a pinwheel of pigeons lifted from the roof of the school and spun across the sky, a swirl of silver against pewter clouds. No artists appeared to be up and about this early on a Sunday, but some of their handiwork was on display in the yard, including a flutter of cloth strips dangling from wire strung between posts, an affair that looked, under the weight of snow, like bedraggled laundry. An inch or two of snow covered the parking lot, and more was falling. Footprints scuffled away from the five or six cars, converged on the sidewalk, then led up to the gate where I had seen the man carrying the bundle of papers. True to form, the Quakers had mounted no sign on the brick gateposts, none on the iron fence, none on the lawn. Twin wreathes tied with red ribbons flanked the porch, and a wind-chime swayed over the front steps. Only when I climbed onto the porch did I see beside the door a small painted board announcing that an "Unprogrammed ('Silent') Meeting" is held here every First Day at 10 A.M., and that "Each person's presence is reason to celebrate."

There was celebration in the face of the woman who greeted me at the door. "So good to see you," she whispered. "Have you worshiped with Quakers before?" I answered with a nod. "Wonderful," she murmured, pointing the way: "We're right in there."

I walked over creaking floorboards from the narrow entrance hall into a living room cluttered with bookshelves, cozy chairs, and exuberant plants. Stacks of pamphlets filled the mantle above a red brick fireplace. Posters on the walls proclaimed various Quaker testimonies, including opposition to the death penalty and a vow against war. It was altogether a busy, frowzy, good-natured space.

From there I entered the former dining room, which had become the meeting room, and I took my seat on a wooden bench near the bay windows. Five other benches were ranged about, facing one another, to form an open square. Before closing my eyes, I noticed that I was the ninth person to arrive. No one spoke. For a long while the only sounds were the scritch of floorboards announcing latecomers, the sniffles and coughs from winter colds, the rumble and whoosh of the furnace, the calling of doves and finches from the eaves. The silence grew so deep that I could hear the blood beating in my ears. I tensed the muscles in my legs, balled up my fists, then let them relax. I tried stilling my thoughts, tried hushing my own inner monologue, in hopes of hearing the voice of God.

That brazen expectation, which grips me now and again, is a steady article of faith for Quakers. They recite no creed, and they have little use for theology, but they do believe that every person may experience direct contact with God. They also believe we are most likely to achieve that contact in stillness, either alone or in the gathered meeting, which is why they use no ministers or music, no readings or formal prayers, no script at all, but merely wait in silence for inward promptings. Quakers are mystics, in other words, but homely and practical ones, less concerned with escaping to heaven than with living responsibly on earth.

The pattern was set in the seventeenth century by their founder, George Fox, who journeyed around England amid civil and ecclesiastical wars, searching for true religion. He did not find it in cathedrals or churches, did not hear it from the lips of priests, did not discover it in art or books. Near despair, he finally encountered what he was seeking within his own depths: "When all my hopes in all men were gone, so that I had nothing outwardly to help me, nor could I tell what to do, then, oh then, I heard a voice which said, 'There is one, even Christ Jesus that can speak to thy condition,' and when I heard it my heart did leap for joy."

My heart was too heavy for leaping, weighed down by thoughts of the unmet miseries all around me. The homeless man shuffled past the House of Pancakes with his trash bag, right down the main street of my brain. I leaned forward on the bench, elbows on knees, listening. By and by there came a flurry of sirens from Meridian, and the sudden ruckus made me twitch. I opened my eyes and took in more of the room. There were twelve of us now, eight women and four men, ranging in age from twenty or so to upwards of seventy. No suits or ties, no skirts, no lipstick or mascara. Instead of dress-up clothes, the Friends wore sweaters or wool shirts in earth colors, jeans or corduroys, boots or running shoes or sandals with wool socks. The wooden benches, buffed and scarred from long use, were cushionless except for a few rectangular scraps of carpet, only one of which had been claimed. A pair of toy metal cars lay nose-to-nose on one bench, a baby's bib and a Bible lay on another, and here and there lay boxes of Kleenex.

Except for those few objects and the benches and people, the room was bare. There was no crucifix hanging on the walls, no saint's portrait, no tapestry, no decoration whatsoever. No candles flickered in shadowy alcoves. The only relief from the white paint were three raised-panel doors that led into closets or other rooms. The only movement, aside from an occasional shifting of hands or legs, was the sashay of lace curtains beside the bay windows when the furnace puffed warm air, and those windows of clear glass provided the only light.

To anyone glancing in from outside, we would have offered a dull spectacle: a dozen grown people sitting on benches, hands clasped in laps or lying open on knees, eyes closed, bodies upright or hunched over, utterly quiet. "And your strength is, to stand still," Fox wrote in one of his epistles, "that ye may receive refreshings; that ye may know, how to wait, and how to walk before God, by the Spirit of God within you." When the refreshing comes, when the Spirit stirs within, one is supposed to rise in the meeting and proclaim what God has whispered or roared. It might be a prayer, a few lines from the Bible or another holy book, a testimony about suffering in the world, a moral concern, or a vision. If the words are truly spoken, they are understood to flow not from the person but from the divine source that upholds and unites all of Creation.

In the early days, when hundreds and then thousands of people harkened to the message of George Fox as he traveled through England, there was often so much fervent speaking in the meetings for worship, so much shaking and shouting under the pressure of the Spirit, that hostile observers mocked these trembling Christians by calling them "Quakers." The humble followers of Fox, indifferent to the world's judgment, accepted the name. They also called themselves Seekers, Children of the Light, Friends in the Truth, and, eventually, the Society of Friends.

Most of these names, along with much of their religious philosophy, derived from the Gospel according to John. There in the first chapter of the recently translated King James Version they could read that Jesus "was the true Light, which lighteth every man that cometh into the world." In the fifteenth chapter they could read Christ's assurance to his followers: "Henceforth I call you not servants; for the servant knoweth not what his lord doeth: but I have called you friends; for all things that I have heard of my Father I have made known unto you."

There was no outward sign of fervor on the morning of my visit to the North Meadow Circle of Friends. I sneezed once, and that was the loudest noise in the room for a long while. In the early years, meetings might go on for half a day, but in our less patient era they usually last about an hour. There is no set ending time. Instead, one of the elders, sensing when the silence has done its work, will signal the conclusion by shaking hands with a neighbor. Without looking at my watch, I guessed that most of an hour had passed, and still no one had spoken.

It would have been rare in Fox's day for an entire meeting to pass without any vocal ministry, as the Quakers call it. But it is not at all rare in our own time, judging from my reading and from my visits to meetings around the country. Indeed, Quaker historians acknowledge that over the past three centuries the Society has experienced a gradual decline in spiritual energy, broken by occasional periods of revival, and graced by many vigorous, God-centered individuals. Quakerism itself arose in reaction to a lackluster Church of England, just as the Protestant Reformation challenged a corrupt and listless Catholic Church, just as Jesus challenged the hidebound Judaism of his day. It seems to be the fate of religious movements to lose energy over time, as direct encounters with the Spirit give way to secondhand rituals and creeds, as prophets give way to priests, as living insight hardens into words and glass and stone.

The Quakers have resisted this fate better than most, but they have not escaped it entirely. Last century, when groups of disgruntled Friends despaired of reviving what they took to be a moribund Society, they split off to form congregations that would eventually hire ministers, sing hymns, read scriptures aloud, and behave for all the world like other low-temperature Protestant churches. In Midwestern states such as Indiana, in fact, these so-called "programmed" Quaker churches have come to outnumber the traditional silent meetings.

I could have gone to a Friends' church in Indianapolis that Sunday morning, but I was in no mood to sit through anybody's program, no matter how artful or uplifting it might be. What I craved was silence—not absolute silence, for I welcomed the ruckus of doves and finches, but rather the absence of human noise. I spend nearly all of my waking hours immersed in language, bound to machines, following streets, obeying schedules, seeing and hearing and touching only what my clever species has made. I often yearn, as I did that morning, to withdraw from all our schemes and formulas, to escape from the obsessive human story, to slip out of my own small self and meet the great Self, the nameless mystery at the core of being. I had a better chance of doing that here among the silent Quakers, I felt, than anywhere else I might have gone.

A chance is not a guarantee, of course. I had spent hundreds of hours in Quaker meetings over the years, and only rarely had I felt myself dissolved away into the Light. More often, I had sat on hard benches rummaging through my past, counting my breaths, worrying about chores, reciting verses in my head, thinking about the pleasures and evils of the day, half hoping and half fearing that some voice not my own would break through to command my attention. It's no wonder that most religions put on a show, anything to fence in the wandering mind and fence out the terror. It's no wonder that only a dozen people would seek out this Quaker meeting on a Sunday morning, while tens of thousands of people were sitting through scripted performances in other churches all across Indianapolis.

Carrying on one's own spiritual search, without maps or guide, can be scary. When I sink into meditation, I often remember the words of Pascal: "The eternal silence of these infinite spaces fills me with dread." What I take him to mean is that the universe is bewilderingly large and enigmatic; it does not speak to us in any clear way; and yet we feel, in our brief spell of life, an urgent desire to learn where we are and why we are and who we are. The silence reminds us that we may well be all on our own in a universe empty of meaning, each of us an accidental bundle of molecules, forever cut off from the truth. If that is roughly what Pascal meant, then I suspect that most people who have thought much about our condition would share his dread. Why else do we surround ourselves with so much noise? We plug in, tune in, cruise around, talk, read, run, as though determined to drown out the terrifying silence of those infinite spaces. The louder this human racket becomes, the more I value those who are willing, like Buddhists and Benedictines and Quakers, to brave the silence.

In the quiet of worship on that snowy First Day, I gradually sank into stillness, down below the babble of thought. Deep in that stillness time let go its grip, the weight of muscle and bone slid away, the empty husk of self broke open and filled with a pure listening.

A car in need of a muffler roared down Talbott Street past the meetinghouse, and the racket hauled me back to the surface of my mind. Only when I surfaced did I realize how far down I had dived. Had I touched bottom? Was there a bottom at all, and if so, was it only the floor of my private psyche, or was it the ground of being?

As I pondered, someone stood up heavily from a bench across

the room from me. Although Quakers are not supposed to care who speaks, I opened my eyes, squinting against the somber snowlight. The one standing was the portly man of whom I had asked the way to the meetinghouse. A ruff of pearl-gray hair fell to his shoulders, a row of pens weighted the breast pocket of his flannel shirt, and the cuffs of his jeans were neatly rolled. He cleared his throat. In times of prayer, he said, he often feels overwhelmed by a sense of the violence and cruelty and waste in the world. Everywhere he looks, he sees more grief. When he complains to God that he's fed up with problems and would like some solutions for a change, God answers that the solutions are for humans to devise. If we make our best effort, God will help. But God isn't going to shoulder the burden for us. We're called not to save the world but to carry on the work of love.

All of this was said intimately, affectionately, in the tone of a person reporting a conversation with a close friend. Having uttered his few words, the speaker sat down. The silence flowed back over us. A few minutes later, he grasped the hand of the woman sitting next to him, and with a rustle of limbs greetings were exchanged all around the room. We blinked at one another, returned from wherever it was we had gone together, separated once more into our twelve bodies. Refreshed, I took up the sack of my self, which seemed lighter than when I had carried it into this room. I looked about, gazing with tenderness at each face, even though I was a stranger to all of them.

A guest book was passed around for signatures. The only visitor besides myself was a man freshly arrived from Louisiana, who laughed about needing to buy a heavier coat for this Yankee weather. An elder mentioned that donations could be placed in a small box on the mantle, if anyone felt moved to contribute. People rose to announce social concerns and upcoming events. After an hour and a half of nearly unbroken silence, suddenly the air filled with talk. It was as though someone had released into our midst a chattering flock of birds.

Following their custom, the Friends took turns introducing themselves and recounting some noteworthy event from the past week. A woman told about lunching with her daughter-in-law, trying to overcome some hard feelings, and about spilling a milkshake in the midst of the meal. A man told how his son's high school basketball coach took the boy out of a game for being too polite toward the opponents. The father jokingly advised his son to scowl and threaten, like the professional athletes whom the coach evidently wished for him to emulate. This prompted a woman to remark that her colleagues at work sometimes complained that she was too honest: "Lie a little, they tell me. It greases the wheels." The only student in the group, a young woman with a face as clear as springwater, told of an English assignment that required her to write about losing a friend. "And I've spent the whole week in memory," she said. A man reported on his children's troubled move to a new school. A woman told of her conversation with a prisoner on death row. Another told of meeting with a union organizer while visiting Mexico. "They're so poor," she said, "we can't even imagine how poor." A woman explained that she and her husband, who cared nothing for football, would watch the Super Bowl that afternoon, because the husband's estranged son from an earlier marriage was playing for the Green Bay Packers. When my turn came, I described hiking one afternoon that week with my daughter, Eva, how we studied the snow for animal tracks, how her voice lit up the woods. Others spoke about cleaning house, going to a concert, losing a job, caring for grandchildren, suffering pain, hearing a crucial story: small griefs, small celebrations.

After all twelve of us had spoken, we sat for one final moment in silence, to mark the end of our time together. Then we rose from those unforgiving benches, pulled on coats, and said our goodbyes. On my way to the door, I was approached by several Friends who urged me to come again, and I thanked them for their company.

As I walked outside into the sharp wind, I recalled how George Fox had urged his followers to "walk cheerfully over the world, answering that of God in every one." There were still no footprints leading to the doors of the art school, no lights burning in the studios. I brushed snow from the windows of my car with gloved hands. To go home, I should have turned south on Meridian, but instead I turned north. I drove slowly, peering into alleys and doorways, looking for the man in the torn jacket with the bulging gray sack over his shoulder. I never saw him, and I did not know what I would have done if I had seen him. Give him a few dollars? Offer him a meal at the International House of Pancakes? Take him home?

Eventually I turned around and headed south, right through the heart of the city. In spite of the snow, traffic was picking up, for the stores recognized no Sabbath. I thought of the eighteenth-century Quaker John Woolman, who gave up shopkeeping and worked modestly as a tailor, so that he would have time for seeking and serving God. "So great is the hurry in the spirit of this world," he wrote in 1772, "that in aiming to do business quickly and to gain wealth the creation at this day doth loudly groan."

In my Quakerly mood, much of what I saw in the capital was

distressing—the trash on curbs, the bars and girlie clubs, the war memorials, the sheer weight of buildings, the smear of pavement, the shop windows filled with trinkets, the homeless men and women plodding along through the snow, the endless ads. I had forgotten that today was Super Bowl Sunday until the woman at meeting spoke of it, and now I could see that half the billboards and marquees and window displays in the city referred to this national festival, a day set aside for devotion by more people, and with more fervor, than any date on the Christian calendar.

"The whole mechanism of modern life is geared for a flight from God," wrote Thomas Merton. I have certainly found it so. The hectic activity imposed on us by jobs and families and avocations and amusements, the accelerating pace of technology, the flood of information, the proliferation of noise, all combine to keep us from that inward stillness where meaning is to be found. How can we grasp the nature of things, how can we lead gathered lives, if we are forever dashing about like water striders on the moving surface of a creek?

By the time I reached the highway outside of Indianapolis, snow was falling steadily and blowing lustily, whiting out the way ahead. Headlights did no good. I should have pulled over until the sky cleared, as the more sensible drivers did. But the snow held me. Rolling on into the whiteness, I lost all sense of motion, lost awareness of road and car. I seemed to be floating in the whirl of flakes, caught up in silence, alone yet not alone, as though I had slipped by accident into the state that a medieval mystic had called the cloud of unknowing. Memory fled, words flew away, and there was only the brightness, here and everywhere.

Notes

Dedication

v

I found this apt description of my friendship with John Elder in *The Best of Meister Eckhart,* ed. Halcyon Backhouse (New York: Crossroad, 1993), p. 143.

Epigraphs

vii

The line from James Wright appears in "The Morality of Poetry," from his *Above the River: The Complete Poems* (New York: Farrar, Straus and Giroux, 1990), p. 60. I quote Peter Matthiessen from *The Snow Leopard* (New York: Viking, 1978), p. 40.

The Force of Spirit

This essay was first delivered at the Orion Society's Millennium Conference, Fire & Grit, in Shepherdstown, West Virginia, on June 23, 1999. My mother-in-law, Dessa Ruth McClure, died on October 26, 1998. At this writing, I'm happy to say, my father-in-law, Earl Morton McClure, though weak, is still among the living.

17–18

Isaiah 40:6–7 (RSV).

Amos and James

> I refrain from citing chapter and verse for the
> numerous quotations from Amos and James
> because those two books are so brief. The essay
> makes clear, I think, where I am quoting from the
> King James Version and where from the Revised
> Standard.

25   Matthew 1:21 (RSV)

36   The words of Jesus about bringing a sword come
>   from Matthew 10:34 (RSV) and those of Paul
>   about the ministry of reconciliation come from 2
>   Corinthians 5:18 (RSV).

Learning
from the Prairie

> Those who would like to learn more about the
> Land Institute or to support their work may write
> to: The Land Institute, 2440 E. Water Well Road,
> Salina, Kansas 67401.

Cabin Dreams

60   Henry Beston, *The Outermost House: A Year of*
>   *Life on the Great Beach of Cape Cod* (New York:
>   Ballantine, 1971), p. 8.

60   Wendell Berry, *The Long-Legged House* (New
>   York: Ballantine, 1969), p. 124.

60   Thomas Merton, *The Hidden Ground of Love* (New York: Farrar, Straus and Giroux, 1985), p. 222.

61   Sue Hubbell, *A Country Year: Living the Questions* (New York: Random House, 1986), p. 12.

62   Harlan Hubbard, *Payne Hollow: Life on the Fringe of Society* (Frankfort, Kentucky: Gnomon Press, 1974), p. 161.

62   Robinson Jeffers, "Tor House," in *Selected Poems* (New York: Vintage, 1965), p. 44.

62   William Butler Yeats, "Meditations in Time of Civil War," in *Collected Poems of W. B. Yeats* (London: Macmillan, 1965), p. 227.

63   Carl Jung, *Memories, Dreams, Reflections,* ed. Aniela Jaffé, trans. Richard and Clara Winston (New York: Vintage, 1963), p. 225.

63   John G. Neihardt, *Black Elk Speaks* (Lincoln: University of Nebraska, 1972), pp. 195–96.

63–64   Annie Dillard, *Pilgrim at Tinker Creek* (New York: Harper's Magazine Press, 1974), pp. 12, 214.

64   Henry David Thoreau, *Walden,* ed. J. Lyndon Shanley (Princeton, New Jersey: Princeton University Press, 1973), pp. 140, 107.

Wood Work

Deryl Dale and Steve Neuenschwander, master carpenters, also appear in my *Writing from the Center* (Bloomington: Indiana University Press, 1995). I'm grateful to them for putting up with my portraits and my carpentry.

71   Genesis 3:17–19 (RSV).

The Power of Stories

84   *Fetching the Dead* (Urbana: University of Illinois Press, 1984).

86   Jared Diamond, *The Third Chimpanzee: The Evolution and Future of the Human Animal* (New York: HarperCollins, 1992), p. 54.

86–87   Italo Calvino, *The Uses of Literature,* trans. Patrick Creagh (New York: Harcourt Brace Jovanovich, 1986), p. 18.

87   Frank O'Connor, *The Lonely Voice: A Study of the Short Story* (New York: Harper, 1985), p. 112.

89   Carol Bly, "Six Uses of Story," Creative Education Literature Catalog (Mankato, Minnesota, 1985), pp. 2–5. See also Carol Bly's *The Passionate, Accurate Story* (Minneapolis: Milkweed, 1990).

89   Tim O'Brien, *The Things They Carried* (New York: Penguin, 1990), p. 204.

90   Henry David Thoreau, *Walden,* ed. J. Lyndon Shan-
          ley (Princeton, New Jersey: Princeton University
          Press, 1973), p. 10.

91   Robert Stone, "The Reason for Stories: Toward a
          Moral Fiction," *Harper's* (June 1988), p. 74.

91   Keith H. Basso, "Stalking with Stories," in Daniel
          Halpern, ed., *On Nature* (Berkeley: North Point,
          1986), pp. 96–97.

93   Eudora Welty, *The Eye of the Story: Selected
          Essays and Reviews* (New York: Vintage, 1979),
          pp. 132–33.

94   "President Designates a Monument Across Utah,"
          New York Times, September 19, 1996, p. A15.

94   Wendell Berry, *Standing by Words* (San Francisco:
          North Point, 1983), pp. 90–91.

94   Leslie Marmon Silko, "Landscape, History, and
          the Pueblo Imagination," in John Elder and Hertha
          D. Wong, eds., *Family of Earth and Sky: Indige-
          nous Tales of Nature from Around the World* (Bos-
          ton: Beacon Press, 1994), p. 254.

95   Richard K. Nelson, "The Embrace of Names,"
          Connotations: The Island Institute Journal, vol. 2,
          no. 2 (fall/winter 1994–95), pp. 8–9.

95   René Dubos, *A God Within* (London: Angus and
          Robertson, 1973), pp. 258–59.

96　　　　　　　Diamond, *The Third Chimpanzee,* p. 123.

96–97　　　　　Ursula K. Le Guin, "The Carrier Bag Theory of
Fiction," in her *Dancing at the Edge of the World:
Thoughts on Words, Women, Places* (New York:
Grove Press, 1989), pp. 165–70.

97　　　　　　　Calvino, *The Uses of Literature,* p. 249.

97　　　　　　　Robert Coles, *The Call of Stories* (Boston:
Houghton Mifflin, 1989), pp. 14, 129.

98　　　　　　　James Baldwin is quoted in Quincy Troupe, ed.,
James Baldwin: The Legacy (New York: Simon
and Schuster, 1989), p. 73.

99　　　　　　　Ursula K. Le Guin, "The Stories We Agree to
Tell," *New York Times Book Review,* March 12,
1995, p. 6.

100　　　　　　*Borges on Writing,* Norman Thomas di Giovanni,
Daniel Halpern, Frank MacShane, eds. (New
York: Dutton, 1973), p. 45.

*Witnessing to a
Shared World*

　　　　　　　　　The two essays of mine referred to here, "Doing
Time in the Thirteenth Chair" and "Wayland,"
appear in *The Paradise of Bombs* (Boston: Beacon
Press, 1991) and *Staying Put* (Boston: Beacon
Press, 1993), respectively.

To Eva, on
Your Marriage

121   1 Timothy 2:11–14 (RSV).

121–22   Mary Wollstonecraft, *A Vindication of the Rights*
                       of Woman (London, 1792), quoted in Miriam
                       Schneir, ed., *Feminism: The Essential Historical*
                       Writings (New York: Vintage, 1994), p. 8.

122   Genesis 1:27–28 (RSV).

122   The words of Jesus on marriage appear in Matthew
                       19: 4–6 and 8 (RSV).

123   Malachi 2:15 (RSV).

123   Proverbs 5:18–19 (RSV).

123   Paul's remarks on marriage appear in Ephesians
                       5:22–24 (RSV).

Hawk Rising

                       The encounter with my dead father in the guise of a
                       red-tailed hawk is one I have written about once
                       before, in "Buckeye," which is collected in my
                       Writing from the Center (Bloomington: Indiana
                       University Press, 1995).

147–48   Edward O. Wilson defines this useful term in *Bio-*
                       philia: The Human Bond with Other Species (Cam-
                       bridge, Massachusetts: Harvard University Press,
                       1984).

Silence

155   George Fox is quoted in Rufus M. Jones, *The Faith and Practice of the Quakers* (Richmond, Indiana: Friends United Press, n.d.), p. 48.

156–57   The epistle of George Fox is quoted in Howard H. Brinton, *The Religious Philosophy of Quakerism* (Wallingford, Pennsylvania: Pendle Hill, 1973), p. 26.

157   John 1:9 and 15:15 (KJV).

160   Blaise Pascal, *Pensées,* trans. A. J. Krailsheimer (Harmondsworth, England: Penguin, 1966), p. 95.

163   George Fox's advice appears in Howard H. Brinton, *Friends for 300 Years* (Wallingford, Pennsylvania: Pendle Hill, 1964), p. 29.

163   *The Journal of John Woolman,* ed. John Greenleaf Whittier (Secaucus, New Jersey: Citadel Press, 1972), p. 211.

164   Thomas Merton, *No Man Is an Island* (New York: Harcourt Brace Jovanovich, 1955), p. 109.

Words of Thanks

Many people had a hand in shaping this book—my teachers, my students, my family and friends, neighbors and editors, as well as thoughtful strangers who wrote me letters after reading something of mine. To all of them, my deep thanks.

I'm grateful to the editors of the following publications, in which earlier versions of essays from this book first appeared: "The Force of Spirit" in *Orion;* "Amos and James" in *Shenandoah* and in *Communion,* ed. David Rosenberg (New York: Anchor Books, 1996); "Heartwood" in *Natural Home;* "Learning from the Prairie" (under the title "Lessons from the Land Institute") and "Hawk Rising" (under the title "Through the Eyes of a Hawk") in *Audubon;* "Cabin Dreams" (under the title "Making a Reader's House a Fit Home") in the *Boston Globe;* "Wood Work" (under the title "Building: Hands to Work") in *Boston College Magazine;* "Father Within" (under the title "Reaching Through My Hands") in *Notre Dame Magazine;* "The Power of Stories" in *The Georgia Review;* "Witnessing to a Shared World" in *A View from the Loft;* "Who Speaks on the Page?" (under the title "From Anonymous, Evasive Prose to Writing with Passion") in *The Chronicle of Higher Education;* "To Eva, on Your Marriage" in *Indiana Alumni Magazine* and in *Fathering Daughters: Reflections by Men,* ed. DeWitt Henry and James Alan McPherson (Boston: Beacon Press, 1998); "To Jesse on Your Marriage" in *Indiana Alumni Magazine;* "Silence" in *Wit-*

ness and in *Falling Toward Grace,* ed. Susan Neville and J. Kent Calder (Bloomington: Indiana University Press, 1998).

To name a few of the editors who encouraged me during the writing of this book, let me thank in particular H. Emerson Blake and George Russell at *Orion,* Mary-Powel Thomas and Lisa Gosselin at *Audubon,* the late Stanley Lindberg at *The Georgia Review,* Kerry Temple at *Notre Dame Magazine,* Judy Schroeder and Lauren Bryant at *Indiana Alumni Magazine,* Karen Winkler at *The Chronicle of Higher Education,* and Deanne Urmy at Beacon Press.

Because I think of essays as a form of deliberate speech, meant to be heard as well as seen, I'm grateful to the organizations and individuals who invited me to try out portions of this book on live audiences: Laurie Lane-Zucker and Marion Gilliam at the Orion Society; Mary Nicolini and the Indiana Teachers of Writing; William Nichols at Denison University and Vassar College; Jeanie Kim at the Lannan Foundation; Jerod Santek at The Loft; Michael Collier at Bread Loaf Writers' Conference; Jim Bailey and Beth Rigel Daugherty at Otterbein College; George Gann and the Society for Ecological Restoration; Patricia Foster at the University of Iowa; Wayne Zade and Rebecca Blair at Westminster College; Carol Holly and Jim Heynen at St. Olaf College; Gary Clark at the Vermont Studio Center; Ronald Nelson at James Madison University; Tony Earley at Vanderbilt University; Dennis Prindle at Ohio Wesleyan University; Larry Smith at Firelands College; Eloise Klein Healy at Antioch-Southern California; Jeffy Gundy at Bluffton College; Stan Tag at Western Washington University; Karla VanderZanden at the San Juan Writers' Workshop; Chris Sprouse at the University of Virginia; Tom Bailey at Western Michigan University and the Association for the Study of Literature and the Environment; Matthew Graham at the Rope Walk Writers' Retreat; Karen Idoine and Michael Yefko at the Rhode Island School of Design; Rita Sizemore Riddle at Radford University; Sandra Kolankiewicz and Stephen Schwartz at Marietta College; John Noffsinger at Norfolk Academy; and Mary Morris at Sarah Lawrence College.

My wise and patient agent, John Wright, has looked after the interests of this writer who lacks all business sense. My colleagues in the Wells Scholars Program at Indiana University— especially Charlene Brown, Patricia Jennings, Theresa Andersen, Amelia Schlegel, Breon Mitchell, James Ackerman, and Perry Metz—have enabled this man without an administrative bone in his body to direct this worthy program with some degree of grace. To the Wells Scholars themselves, whose names I carry close to my heart, I give thanks for their inspiring company.

Wes Jackson and Joan Olsen offered me generous hospitality during my visit to the Land Institute in Salina, Kansas. Members of the North Meadow Circle of Friends in Indianapolis graciously opened their worship to this quiet and observant visitor. Hank Lentfer of Gustavus, Alaska, shared with me the sacred waters of Glacier Bay. My thanks to all of them.

This book is dedicated to a brilliant teacher, writer, and conservationist, whose friendship has nourished me now for a dozen years.

Finally, I thank my dear Ruth, who reminds me where the center is, and I thank Eva and Jesse, who've taught me more than they will ever know. With Ruth, I welcome our new kinship with Eva's husband, Matthew Lee Allen, and his parents, Don and Charlene Allen; and our new kinship with Jesse's wife, Caroline Dean Parkinson, and her parents, George and Rosalind Parkinson.